SIBERIAN HUSKY

OWNER'S GUIDE™

FROM THE EDITORS OF DOGFANCY. MAGAZINE

CONTENTS

Siberian Husky, a Smart Owner's Guide™
part of the Kennel Club Books® Interactive Series™
ISBN: 978-1593787-80-6. ©2010

Kennel Club Books Inc., 40 Broad St., Freehold, NJ 07728. Printed in China.
All rights reserved. No part of this book may be reproduced in any form,
by Photostat, scanner, microfilm, xerography or any other means, or incorporated
into any information retrieval system, electronic or mechanical,
without the written permission of the copyright owner.

*photographers include Isabelle Francias/BowTie Inc.; Tara Darling/BowTie Inc.;
Gina Cioli and Pamela Hunnicutt/BowTie Inc. Cover dog: Max, owned
by Carlos and Brenda Ramos in Southern California.*

For CIP information, see page 176.

K9 EXPERT

If you have added a Siberian Husky to your family from a responsible breeder or a rescue group — or are planning to do so — congratulations! You have fallen in love with one of the most handsome and devoted breeds in all of dogdom.

Most fans of the breed are first seduced by the Siberian's haunting eyes, but this dog is more than a good-looking, blue-eyed hunk. In fact, the Siberian's eyes are not always blue. Brown eyes are equally common, as are dogs with one blue and one brown eye.

Besides his dramatic appearance, the Siberian is friendly, alert and energetic. Of course, no breed is perfect for every house-hold so prospective owners need to be accepting of the Siberian's idiosyncrasies.

This breed is incredibly gregarious and social. He needs the company of other dogs and his people pretty constantly. If you work all day, a second dog to keep him company would be a good plan. The Siberian also makes a terrible watch dog. While some Working Group breeds are one-man dogs, the Siberian loves everyone.

Whether your preference is for a black, gray or red dog with white markings — or even a solid white — this breed will put your vacuum cleaner to the test at least once a year when he sheds hair all over the house. Many owners prefer this annual coat blow to the year-round shedding of many other smooth-coated breeds.

On the downside, the Siberian can be a digging fool. If gardening is a hobby of yours,

The Siberian Husky is a majestic breed that really brings out dogdom's link to wild wolves.

be sure to segregate the plants and shrubs. Having a garden and a dog are not mutually exclusive but you will have to be resourceful if you expect your Siberian to share the backyard.

While affectionate with humans and social with other dogs, the Siberian still maintains predatory instincts and demonstrates them around small animals in and around the house, including cats, birds and rodents. If you keep these furry critters, you will have to protect them from the Sibe's swift and sneaky hunting skills.

The Siberian adapts well to most suburban settings because he is a medium-sized dog. According to the American Kennel Club breed standard, males range from 21 inches to 23½ inches at the shoulder and 45 to 60 pounds; females reach 20 to 22 inches at the shoulder and 45 to 50 pounds. The standard has disqualifications in place to ensure that size does not creep up and compromise the breed's agility on the trail.

While a reasonable size, the Siberian's need for speed cannot be denied. He has a tremendous desire to run, and he must have this outlet but within safe, controlled boundaries. The Sibe is stubborn and independent so it falls on you to save him from himself. Sledding comes naturally to the breed and is the ideal way to let him burn off energy. During the dryer months in temperate climates, wheeled carts provide the Sibe an opportunity to pull in harness and continue a fitness regime all year long.

To see this breed joyfully pulling a sled is to witness him connecting with his time-honored past. It acknowledges tradition while giving your devoted companion much-

JOIN OUR ONLINE Club Husky™

With this Smart Owner's Guide™, you are well on your way to getting your husky diploma.

But your Siberian Husky education doesn't end here.

You're invited to join in **Club Husky™ (DogChannel.com/Club-Husky)**, a FREE online site with lots of fun and instructive features such as:

◆ **forums, blogs** and **profiles** where you can connect with other husky owners

◆ **downloadable charts** and **checklists** to help you be a smart and loving Siberian Husky owner

◆ access to Siberian Husky **e-cards** and **wallpapers**

◆ interactive **games**

◆ canine **quizzes**

The **Smart Owner's Guide** series and **Club Husky** are backed by the experts at DOG FANCY® magazine and DogChannel.com — who have been providing trusted and up-to-date information about dogs and dog people for more than 40 years. Log on and join the club today!

needed exercise. Provide the Siberian a safe, happy outlet and you will be richly rewarded with a beautiful, steadfast friend to all of your family.

Allan Reznik,
Editor-at-Large, DOG FANCY

& BEAUTIFUL

The Siberian Husky has earned respect and an honest reputation throughout the world and across time. In northeast Siberia (Russia) and Alaska, this Northern breed has long been admired for his ability to travel long distances and transport loads through the snow. Even today, credit is given to this dog that goes the extra mile — whether he is a sled dog or stay-at-home pet.

So what are the Siberians' traits that have won the hearts of sporting individuals and dog lovers alike, both then and now? Notable enthusiasts reveal the numerous facets of this breed's highly complex personality and how it can befriend a human or another dog for an eternity.

SIBERIAN SMARTS

Siberian Husky breeder Pam Thomas of Elkhorn, Wisc., knows first and foremost that Siberians are alert and intelligent. "They are problem solvers," she says. "They can actually solve problems."

Did You Know?

Sleep is important to dogs; they do it for 12 to 14 hours a day. Studies have shown that people who sleep with their dog are less rested than those who keep their dog in her own bed. It is a known fact that a 35-pound husky can take up three-quarters of a king-sized bed. The best plan is for you to have your place while your dog has hers.

Thomas recalls one day when three of her Siberian Huskies were out in the backyard playing. "We had fenced off a new piece of grass so they couldn't dig it up again," she says. "One of the dogs got her rabies tag caught in the chicken wire [fence]. She tugged and tugged on it but couldn't get it off."

Nikko, another playmate and witness to this dilemma, came to the rescue. The 3-year-old dog walked over and yanked the tag a few times. Again, no success. She then leapt over the chicken wire [fence] and released the hook off the wire so that her Siberian pal was free. That's just one feat of the smart Siberian Husky.

WANTS TO BE INDEPENDENT

Most Siberian Husky owners realize that this Northern breed is also independent. In other words, Siberians are self reliant. If you're looking for a one-person dog (such as a Brittany Spaniel), you had better keep looking, because the Siberian Husky's free spirit will leave you howling. Siberians look out for No. 1.

"He's a one-dog dog and that dog is himself," says Siberian Husky breeder Del Goetz, owner of Wolfpack Kennels in Marin, Calif. "Yet he's wise enough to know that his survival depends on interaction with his pack.

The Siberian Husky will create his own well-rounded pack in his pursuit of happiness."

That means they're good with dogs, as well as people, be it a romp in the dog park or a trek in the snow. The wrinkle is that a Siberian doesn't care if you go along or not. Nic Matulich, rescue coordinator of the Bay Area Siberian Husky Club of Campbell, Calif., explains: "I can have one of my friends come over and say, 'Can I borrow this dog, this dog and that dog? And my Siberians would be out the door and in his car in a second."

Some devoted Siberian Husky owners will even admit their dogs lack "passionate loyalty." It's not a big problem, though. Siberians have enough nonloyal passion to go around for everybody.

LOVES TO BE SOCIAL

OK, the Siberian isn't the ever-loyal Labrador or poodle. However, this outgoing dog doesn't fear strangers, be it the postman or pizza boy, and he greets guests and other dogs with open and welcome paws. In other words, there are no barkers here — just a very friendly and pack-oriented pal.

◆ **Very Friendly Fidos:** True, the husky is a worthless watchdog — definitely not the breed to be counted on to participate in the neighborhood watch group. He will, how-

Did You Know? When your husky is an adolescent (between 9 months and 1 year of age), her ancient lupine heritage may nudge her to make a bid for leadership in the home. It's also during this time when aggressive behavior can develop if the owners do not respond appropriately to the challenge. During this period, it's important that you be particularly steadfast. If your dog seems to be dominant toward only one person in the family, let that person take over the feeding and walking duties, if possible. This will help create a trusting bond between that person and your Siberian.

Meet other Siberian owners just like you. On our Siberian forums, you can chat about your Siberian Husky and ask other owners for advice on training, health issues and anything else about your favorite dog breed. Log onto **DogChannel.com/Club-Husky** for details!

ever, *watch* a house burglar take your TV, stereo and, as the burglar walks out the door, will remind him that "you forgot the jewelry in the bedroom." It's simply part of the breed's good-nature.

"One of the most important things is that Siberians are very affectionate and loving," Goetz says. "They're very sensitive. If I've had a bad day and they knew I was stressed, they would be very solicitous of me and lick my face. They know when love is needed because they are sensitive."

◆ **Pack-Oriented Pooches:** Not only are Siberian Huskies people lovers but they are also dog lovers. "They are innately pack-oriented," Thomas says. "If you watch a group of Siberians that has been raised together, the dogs function like a pack — just like a wolf pack."

Goetz agrees. She has studied her Siberian Huskies over the years by closely monitoring their unique domestic dog pack conduct. No doubt, her domestic pack of American Kennel Club purebred dogs actually behaves uncannily the same as wolves do in the wild.

A researcher at heart, since 1978 Goetz has noticed wolf-life resemblances in her pack of Siberian Huskies while training them for show, obedience and sled-dog

Siberians need freedom to run around and explore. A mile of exercise every other day might be enough to keep them calm and fulfilled. On the other hand, if you run your dog five miles, don't expect him to stay quietly in the house while you go to work. He will be pumped up and somewhat upset about suddenly being alone. There will be no place for him to go but through the wall!

— dog trainer Steve Diller from Westchester, N.Y.

racing. As she spoke with other dog enthu-siasts who also owned large groups of dogs, she quickly learned that she, too, was the owner of something quite incredi-ble. The behavior of dogs in a pack is very different from the behavior of one or two dogs in a family household. Some canine observers believe that when dogs are among other dogs in a group, their senses are heightened to such a degree that they demonstrate more feral behavior.

TENDS TO BE STRONG WILLED

The Siberian Husky has been called "stubborn" and "headstrong" by some, which overlap with his independent nature and extraordinary intelligence. "The best way to explain this is to do so with a description of the sled-dog team," Matulich says. "You have a sled dog that is working up front, a driver in the back. If the driver is telling him to go forward and there's a haz-ard [on the trail], be it a crevice or thin ice, the dog has to be able to disobey the driver." That's where the Siberian's strong will can be a godsend.

Siberians also learn things quickly "but if you keep drilling them, they'll become bored," Matulich says. "You may never get them to do it again, just simply because

The Siberian Husky needs plenty of outdoor time to burn off his excess energy.

Proper kenneling, fencing and strategic landscaping combined with exercise, attention and supervision can prevent your husky from becoming part of the estimated one-in-three dogs who gets lost during her lifetime, most of who never finds her way home.

they have an obstinate streak in them for avoiding boredom."

Playing with toys may be the key. Then again, maybe not. Sometimes Siberian Huskies want the toy that they want and they're not going to let you have it. If you try to get it, they're going to get it back.

LOVES TO RUN

Of all the traits common in the Siberian, the most well known is this Northern breed's desire to run. Why the need to run? According to some breed experts, this need can be explained in one word: genetics. It's in their blood, they say. Others claim the Siberian to be instinctually territorial, and given the opportunity, he will roam long distances to build a territory.

Goetz recalls the one time two of her Siberians did just that. As the story goes, her tenant had inadvertently left the back gate open and two of Goetz's dogs escaped from the confines of her yard. The duo headed for Muir Woods, a nearby park.

When Goetz called the park rangers and inquired about her wayward dogs, they casually reported, "Oh yeah, we saw Flower and Chudtka crossing the parking lot about 10 minutes ago." Knowing where this course would take her dogs, Goetz proceeded to Muir Beach. Passersby told her that "the dogs went that-a-way" as they pointed in the

direction of the pair's paw prints in the sand. "I then saw them go up the hill in the distance," Goetz recalls. "I was shouting at them in the wind, but they didn't hear me."

So Goetz followed the two down the highway … yet still no dogs. Frustrated, she gave up the chase and headed home, and there, innocently sitting at the gate were her two adventuring Siberians. "They did a 13½-mile loop in less than two hours," Goetz says.

Thomas has caught her Siberians on the run, too. She says they'll take the puppies out on the trail, so they can watch the big dogs getting hooked up to the sled. "When the team leaves the yard, we turn the puppies loose," Thomas says. "They will run half a mile trying to catch up."

THWARTING THE ESCAPE ARTIST

Since the Siberian Husky ranks as one of dogdom's most skilled escape artists, you will need to know how to keep him from hitting the road. Kennel and yard fencing materials vary widely, with some working better than others for confining a husky. Here are some common examples.

◆ **Aluminum:** Most of today's wrought-iron-looking fences are actually aluminum. Sold in a number of eye-catching designs and colors, aluminum affords a serviceable fence that adds class to any home.

Siberian Huskies aren't dogs that like to sit around. They are always looking for a place to run.

◆ **Chain Link:** This woven wire fencing gives rather than bends upon moderate impact, helping it maintain shape and appearance. Available in different thicknesses, or gauges, chain link is a favorite for kennels and perimeter fencing.

◆ **Landscape Fences:** Thick hedges and bushes with 2- to 3-foot high wire or plastic fencing hidden at the base can make a surprisingly effective, neighbor-friendly barrier, which is particularly valuable in "no-fence" areas.

◆ **Underground electric:** Useful in no-fence areas or on large properties, underground fences employ a collar that delivers an electric shock when a dog crosses the wire. These provide limited security unless combined with a physical fence.

◆ **Vinyl:** Vinyl fencing has become widespread in recent years. Sold in several colors, vinyl fencing usually comes in 4- to 5-foot long panels that require a stepped placement on sloping ground. Beautiful and low maintenance, vinyl offers an excellent fencing option.

◆ **Welded Wire:** Very thick wire that's securely welded makes an excellent kennel. Thinner gauged, welded-wire fencing, often used for livestock, can bend when a dog jumps against it.

◆ **Wood:** Treated lumber, cedar and redwood present popular choices for fencing. Attractive and workable into many styles, wood provides a strong barrier against escape-prone huskies.

Your Siberian Husky is probably a big fan of cold weather. Unless you live in Antarctica, chances are she'll have to tolerate warmer temperatures for at least part of the year. Keep her cool during those dog days with these tips:

■ Provide supervised access to a plastic kiddie pool filled with water.

■ Buy several bags of ice and make a big ice pile for her to play in.

■ Set up a sprinkler on your lawn and let her run through.

■ Make a cool spot in your yard where she is allowed to dig.

■ Fill stuffable dog toys with kibble moistened in beef or chicken-flavored water and freeze them. Then, give your dog the resulting "toysicles."

DIFFICULT NOT TO LOVE

Despite his desires to run free, the Siberian Husky most of all captures the hearts of people everywhere. Perhaps it's his free spirit and energy that dog lovers admire. With his brains, autonomy, gentle spirit, perseverance and zest for life, who could resist the lovable Siberian Husky?

NOTABLE & QUOTABLE

Most behavioral problems occur if the dog is bored or neglected. Give him something to do. Huskies need daily exercise, but this is not a high-energy dog. My dogs do fine with a couple of hours a day in a large fenced yard.
— breeder Judy Russell from Davisburg, Mich.

JOIN OUR ONLINE Club Husky™

Show your artistic side. Share photos, videos and artwork of your favorite breed on Club Husky. You can also submit jokes, riddles and even poetry about Siberian Huskies. Browse through our various galleries and see the talent of fellow Siberian owners. Go to **DogChannel.com/Club-Husky** and click on "Galleries" to get started.

Psychic Dog Pack

According to Del Goetz, owner of Wolfpack Kennels in Marin, Calif., her Siberians can often sense upcoming natural events, such as thunderstorms and earthquakes. Goetz adamantly proclaims the validity of these predictions, and supposedly, these dogs' sensory capabilities have been right on the mark.

Within a pack, a Siberian Husky's behavior becomes more complex prior to these natural phenomena, especially before an earthquake. Throughout the years, Goetz has distinguished between the dog's various behaviors, and as a result, is able to predict whether it is an earthquake or a thunderstorm that is affecting the dogs' moods.

Ever since the Oct. 17, 1989, Loma Prieta earthquake that rumbled through the San Francisco Bay area, Goetz believes her dogs' behavior — from an increase in activity to more poop than usual! — may be a way to predict if an earthquake is going to hit and at what magnitude.

Claiming that she has an estimated 60- to 75-percent success rate for earthquake prediction, Goetz also says her Siberians give a 100-percent accurate weather report if a thunderstorm is building on the distant horizon. "I've found that if a thunderstorm is coming our way, the dogs get nervous and show a lot more nervous energy," she says. "They'll be more active, argumentative and aggressive toward one another." The dogs also want to be inside and close to Goetz.

Is dog pack behavior a reliable weather predictor? John C. Wright, Ph.D., a professor of psychology at Mercer University in Macon, Ga., answers: "It's probably true that the dogs are detecting something before we are, but that can be explained just by the fact that some of the dogs' senses are a little more efficient at low-stimulus levels than ours."

Wright adds that a phenomenon called "social facilitation" can be applied to Goetz's pack of Siberians. This term simply means that when a dog is doing something that he normally does easily, he will do it more effectively in the presence of another dog. The pack environment increases the dog's abilities.

Siberian Huskies may be independent, but they are not loners. They enjoy being around other dogs and people.

THE SIBERIAN IN SHORT

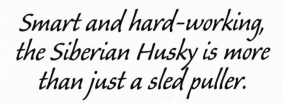

Smart and hard-working, the Siberian Husky is more than just a sled puller.

COUNTRY OF ORIGIN: Russia (Siberia)

WHAT HIS FRIENDS CALL HIM: Balto, Denali, Mushy, Yukon Jack

SIZE: standing 20 to 23½ inches at the shoulders, weighing 45 to 60 pounds

COAT & COLOR: double coat, medium length, straight outer, dense under. Any color ranging from black to white with a variety of markings.

PERSONALITY TRAITS: This breed is known to be active, lively, friendly, outgoing and independent. They make wonderful family dogs but are not one-person dogs.

WITH KIDS: Siberian Huskies are good with children, but it is best when the child's energy level matches the dog's.

WITH OTHER ANIMALS: This breed is good with other dogs but not with smaller household pets.

ENERGY LEVEL: high

EXERCISE NEEDS: Adequate exercise is a must, to burn off excess energy.

GROOMING NEEDS: Siberian Huskies shed heavily multiple times a year and need to be brushed about three times a week.

TRAINING NEEDS: These very intelligent dogs enjoy the challenge of learning new things.

LIVING ENVIRONMENT: These are not city dogs; they need a fenced yard in a suburban or rural area.

LIFESPAN: 12 or more years

HISTORY

Several thousand years ago, primitive Eskimo-like tribes in Siberia, Russia, used dogs for specific functions in everyday life. These dogs were essential to the humans' survival as they performed vital tasks, which included accompanying the hunters, scenting trails and helping to transport food back to the villages. Each tribe had its own specific type, which at this point was a precursor to a specific breed of dog, but all of the Northern dogs were similar in the sense of being jackal-type dogs that, at one time, had been crossbred with Arctic wolves. Of course, this was thousands of years ago, and through careful breeding and maintenance of pure bloodlines, the "wolf" was bred out of the dog. The purebred Siberian Husky of today is not a wild wolf hybrid, as anyone close to the breed will attest, but a beautiful, friendly, tractable, wonderful dog in pet and working capacities.

In Siberia, the ancestors of the husky were originally used for hunting — until another use for them evolved. Each tribe bred and maintained its own specific type of dog. These Northern dogs eventually evolved into the distinct breeds that we know today: Alaskan Malamute, American Eskimo Dog and Samoyed, to name a few.

The Chukchi tribe is credited with the origination of the dog that we have come to know as the Siberian Husky. The Chukchis inhabited the part of Siberia closest to Alaska, at a time when the climate was not so harsh. When weather conditions changed for the worse, the tribe was forced to venture farther from their settlement to find food. The tribe lived inland, but they came to depend on the sea for food. Thus arose the necessity for a method of transporting the food over the considerable distance, and the sled became that ever-important method of transport. Hence, the "sled dog" was born! In addition to accompanying the tribesmen to the sea and bringing home food, the sled dogs were used for transporting goods and trading between tribes, and for hauling the tribe's possessions if they had to relocate to a more hospitable region.

The husky, then referred to as the Siberian Chukchi, or simply the Chukchi, was bred mainly for endurance rather than for speed or strength. The dogs were bred specifically to pull light loads at medium speeds; heavier loads required teams of dogs. The most important trait was that they were able to withstand the long distances and transport their cargo intact. The dogs had to be very energy efficient in that they had to perform their task with as little effort as possible; they needed to have energy left over to keep their bodies warm in the below-freezing temperatures.

The Chukchi were meticulous in their maintenance of the dogs' pure bloodlines. Only the best male lead dogs were bred; the

it's a Fact

"Husky" is a generic term referring to any Northern-type snow dog. It derives from a bastardization of the word "Eskie" for Eskimo; the Eskimos continue to depend on sled dogs for survival.

rest of the males were castrated. The dogs had to have almost endless endurance, superb scenting ability, thick woolly coats to protect from the harsh climate, extreme tractability and willingness to obey. The breed today is recognized as one of the friendliest, and is especially known for being good with children. This has much to do with how the tribespeople treated the dogs. The Chukchi women and children were responsible for the dogs' daily care, so the dogs adapted to family life and became accustomed to much interaction with humans. The children were encouraged to play with the dogs. Today, Huskies are regarded as excellent family pets — very playful and always ready to make a new friend.

RUSSIAN INVASION

Although originated in Siberia, the Siberian Husky is generally thought of as an American breed since it was in Alaska that these dogs first gained recognition as a separate breed rather than just another type of Arctic dog. Before their introduction to America via Alaska, which at that time was not yet a state, huskies were favored by Russian explorers, who brought the dogs along while charting the Siberian coastline. Still known as Chukchis, the dogs were brought to Alaska in late 1908 by a Russian fur trader named Goosak to be entered in the inaugural All-Alaska Sweepstakes, a 408-mile sled–dog race with a $10,000 first prize. The locals were unimpressed by Goosak's dogs; they were small in comparison to the sled dogs they were used to seeing. Goosak persuaded a driver named Louis Thrustrup to lead his team and, despite tremendous odds against them, the team placed a close third.

This first sweepstakes race was just the beginning. Dog-sled racing as a sport was becoming very popular, and the Siberian dogs quickly earned a reputation as top-notch sled dogs. Following this race, a Scotsman by the name of Fox Maule Ramsay was so taken with the Chukchi dogs that he chartered a boat to cross the Bering Sea to Siberia and returned with more than 60 of the best Arctic dogs he could find. In the third All-Alaska race, two teams of Ramsay's dogs placed first and second. Ramsay himself was the driver of the second-place team.

A very well-known story that documents the Siberian Husky's unparalleled skill as a sled dog is the story of what has come to be known as the "great serum run" of 1925. An outbreak of diphtheria in Nome, Alaska, necessitated the delivery of antitoxin to prevent further spread of the disease, yet severe weather conditions made it impossible to transport it by air. The nearest supply of serum, which was in Anchorage, could be

Did You Know?

Huskies are well known for being very clean. Although they shed, this is not a hygiene problem. Instead, they maintain their own cleanliness and have surprisingly little "doggie" smell. They are also easy to groom. Although that thick coat may look intimidating, all they need is brushing; no special grooming is required for the show ring. Keep in mind that the double coat of the Siberian will mat and become very unkempt if not brushed regularly. No matter how fastidious your husky is, she simply cannot groom her entire coat, especially the parts that she cannot crane her neck to reach.

transported by rail only as far as the town of Nenana, but there were still more than 650 miles to travel to reach Nome. The only feasible way to cover the remaining distance, it seemed, was to use teams of sled dogs. The relay teams covered the distance in just five-and-a-half days, which was a remarkably short time to cover such a distance, and the serum was delivered to Nome in time to save the people from what would have otherwise resulted in certain death.

Word of the dogs' incredible endurance and heroism in the face of below-freezing temperatures and blizzard-like conditions spread quickly. The names of the dogs and their drivers became household words. Two drivers in particular, Gunnar Kasan and Leonard Seppala, who used teams of Siberian Huskies, became especially well known. Kasan's team was the last relay team, the team that delivered the serum to Nome on Feb. 2, 1925.

Kasan's lead dog, named Balto, had already proven his worth as a sled dog and scenter many times over, but after this adventure, he became recognized as the finest lead dog in Alaska. In fact, today a statue of Balto stands in New York City's Central Park as a symbol of the serum relay and to commemorate all of the fine dogs that participated. Seppala and his team garnered recognition for covering more than 300 miles on the journey to Nome, the

longest distance covered by any single team in the relay.

ESTABLISHMENT OF THE BREED

Following the serum relay, Seppala toured the United States with a group of dogs, most of them Siberian Huskies, to give sled-dog demonstrations. At this time, the word "husky" was used as a generic name for all of the sled-dog breeds. The Chukchi dog was first given the name "Siberian Husky" by Americans. These demonstrations gave the Arctic dogs widespread exposure and sparked interest in the Siberian. There was even a sled-dog demonstration at the 1932 Olympic Games in Lake Placid, N.Y. After completing his exhibition tour, Seppala settled in New

it's a **Fact** Since 1967, huskies have impressed the world at the Iditarod Great Sled Race, the world's longest sled-dog event, stretching across Alaska for 1,049 miles.

Today, the most famous Siberian Husky of all time, Balto, is immortalized as a statue in NYC's Central Park as a testament to the breed's brave and heroic temperament.

Just how quickly will your Siberian Husky puppy grow? Go to Club Husky and download a growth chart. You also can see your puppy's age in human years. The old standard of multiplying your dog's age by seven isn't quite accurate. Log onto **DogChannel.com/Club-Husky** and click on "Downloads."

England and started racing extensively with his dogs. Not only did he establish himself as a top sled-dog driver but he also helped establish the Siberian Husky in the eastern United States through his own breeding program. Seppala bred his dogs, and they became foundation stock for other New England breeders. The Seppala name is known by everyone involved in huskies today; in fact, all American-Kennel-Club-registered Siberian Huskies can be traced back to Seppala bloodlines.

New England became home to a concentration of quality Siberian Husky kennels, Arthur Walden's Chinook Kennels in New Hampshire being one of the most important. Walden had already been breeding sled dogs when Seppala arrived with his huskies. Again, these dogs were smaller than those that were being produced in the area, and people immediately discounted their skill as sled dogs. However, as soon as the dogs started racing, people took notice. Seppala's dogs

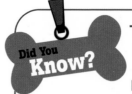

Did You Know?

The Siberian Husky, like all other Northern breeds of dog, boasts a full brush tail that is carried over the dog's back. Although the standard does not state why this is an important characteristic of the Siberian Husky, evolution does. This abundantly coated brush tail could easily protect the husky's face from snow and wind when the dog curls up on the ground. This type of tail, therefore, is a vital component for a dog destined to work and sleep outdoors in Arctic conditions.

consistently, and handily, beat the local dogs in sled races. Walden, with the help of Milton and Eva "Short" Seeley, produced quality Siberian Huskies based on the

The Northern breeds of dog, typified by the Siberian Husky, share many physical characteristics, including the prick, well-furred ears; brush curled tails; thick double coats and pointy muzzles. Among the celebrated Northern breeds, we have the Alaskan Malamute, Samoyed, Finnish Spitz, Akita and American Eskimo Dog. In addition to pulling sleds, Northern dogs earned their daily fish by hunting, herding and guarding the family.

Alaskan stock, some of which came directly from Seppala.

Lorna Demidoff established the prominent Monadnock Kennel, also in New England. Her first champion was a dog she acquired from Chinook, and she followed with many homebred champions and top racing dogs. It is important to note that Demidoff and Seeley were not only top breeders but top sled-dog drivers as well. In fact, they are two of the top women drivers of all time.

The focus of the New England kennels was to preserve the Siberian Husky's working ability while producing dogs that were an esthetically pleasing and could win in the conformation ring. The Chukchis' breeding program focused on function rather than form; for example, the dog's beautiful woolly coats were intended to insulate the dogs' bodies, not to be admired by show fanciers. The tribe needed the dogs for survival; they had no need for a beautiful dog. Dog fanciers, however, with intense interest in showing dogs as well as racing them, wanted the best of both worlds; they wanted the best-quality and best-looking dogs possible. Even with an emphasis on beauty, the New England kennels still managed to consistently produce dogs that were some of the finest racing sled-dogs around.

SMART TIP!

While your Siberian Husky will adapt to very cold temperatures, excessive heat may bother her. Remember the Arctic climate from whence she comes — she's well suited for snow and ice, not for heat and humidity. Keep that in mind and always give your husky access to shade and fresh water. Never leave your dog in a parked car in warm weather. Dogs of Northern descent have practically no tolerance for heat and will succumb to heat stroke within a very short time.

OFFICIAL RECOGNITION

The breed was recognized as the Siberian Husky by the AKC in 1930; the first AKC-registered Siberian was named Fairbanks Princess Chena. The breed is also recognized by America's second-oldest registry, the United Kennel Club. The UKC originally used the name "Artic Husky" but changed it to "Siberian Husky" in 1991. Today, the breed is still refered to as the Artic Husky in the United Kingdom, although the breed's official name worldwide is Siberian Husky.

Did You Know?

The Siberian Husky is very different from other breeds, retaining a great deal of her ancestors' wolfish ways. Unlike retrievers, pointers, shepherds, terriers and toy dogs, which have had most of the pack orientation bred out of them, the primitive, highly intelligent Siberian Husky retains an extremely strong pack mentality. This mindset must be understood and honored by her owners. While a dog pack is assuredly not the same thing as a wolf pack, neither is it altogether different.

You have an unbreakable bond with your dog, but do you always understand her? Go online and download "Dog Speak," which outlines how dogs communicate. Find out what your Siberian Husky is saying when she barks, howls or growls. Go to **DogChannel.com/ Club-Husky** and click on "Downloads."

Jack London Calls

American author Jack London (1876-1918) wrote about brutal men and manwise dogs who learned how to adapt and survive in the best and worst of times. As a novelist, London's main reputation continues to depend on his two best-known wolf-dog (mostly Siberian Husky) books: *The Call of the Wild* (1903) and *White Fang* (1906). London experts believe the author had a tendency to see himself as part animal: He signed his intimate letters "Wolf," named his mansion "Wolf House," owned a husky called "Brown Wolf" and had a wolf's head as a bookplate.

His three fictional wolf-dogs — Buck, Fang and Brown Wolf, the title character in a short story by the same name, which first appeared in *Everybody's Magazine* in August 1906 — indeed possess some typical Siberian Husky temperament traits.

BUCK

But he is not always alone. When the long winter nights come on and the wolves follow their meat into the lower valleys, he may be seen running at the head of the pack through the pale moonlight or glimmering bore-alis, leaping gigantic above his fellows, his great throat a-bellow as he sings a song of the Younger World which is the song of the pack.

— The Call of the Wild

Buck was drawn from the author's northland experiences, according to the late London collector, authority and biographer, Russ Kingman. "[London's] tent was pitched next to Marshall and Louis Bond's cabin. [London] loved the Bond's dog, named Jack, more than any other dog he had owned. I figure every day [London] would go down and get the mail in Dawson City, and my guess is that Jack always went with him."

Later, the friendship grew so much that [London] eternalized the Bond's dog in the character Buck. "Most dog stories are mushy, but this one is just a story of a dog," Kingman points out. A lot of critics also say Buck's character is based on a dramatization of Jack's free-spirited days spent tramping in Niagara Falls to doing time in the Erie County Penitentiary in Buffalo, N.Y.

BROWN WOLF

Wolf's perturbation began to wax. He desired ubiquity. He wanted to be in two places at the same time, with the old master and the new, and steadily the distance between them was increasing. He sprang about excitedly, making short nervous leaps and twists, now toward one, now toward the other, in painful indecision, not know-ing his own mind, desiring both and unable to choose, uttering quick sharp whines and beginning to pant.

— "Brown Wolf"

Not only did Jack, the Bond's dog, influence London's Alaskan adven-tures, so did Brown, a wolf-dog (Siberian mix) from the northland. Take a look at Kingman's research notes: "Alaskan wolf-dog, a true husky brown and white with a furry coat. He even had a limp to show his days in harness on the Yukon trails. His mas-ter had been an old sourdough. On his death his retainers asked [London] to take Brown. They were strangers but knew of his Klondike days. He said 'yes,' but Brown said 'no.' After many trips to bring him back, [London] finally gave up ... Lo and behold, Brown had decided that [London] was okay and adopted him completely."

[London] later paid tribute to the wolf-dog and created "Brown Wolf," in which a stray dog, months later, recognizes and follows his owner from the northland.

WHITE FANG

White Fang is left inside the cabin. As the two men head down to the boat, they hear White Fang howling as though his master was dead. He is voicing utter woe. His cry [burst] upward in great heartbreaking crushes, dying down into quavering misery ..."

— White Fang

White Fang is the "complete antithesis (and) companion piece" to The Call of the Wild. London wrote, "I'm going to reverse the process." The result? The key canine character White Fang is three-fourth wolf and one-part dog and was given memorable traits of domesticity, faithfulness, love and morality.

While writing the story, London owned a dog named Glen. In his essay "The Other Animals" (Collier's, September 1908) he wrote: "His father was Brown, a wolf-dog that had been brought down from Alaska, and his mother was a half-wild mountain shepherd dog...." In "The Other Animals," the author also claimed dogs can think, but that they are "not directed by abstract reasoning, but by instinct, sensation, and emotion and by sim-ple reasoning."

CHAPTER 3

SELECTING

A SIBERIAN

As rough and tumble as the Siberian Husky can be, nothing is cuter than a husky puppy. His sweet face and round little body inspire *oohs* and *ahhs* from all who see him. That wonderful endearing quality, however, can also distract you from taking the time and doing the legwork necessary to find a puppy who's not only adorable but also healthy in body and temperament. The key to finding the best Siberian Husky puppy for you is to resist being charmed into a hasty decision and wait to find a responsible breeder. Then, you can have fun picking just the right puppy from a litter of those lovable faces.

You're going to have your Siberian Husky for 12 or more years, so the time you spend early on to locate a healthy, well-adjusted puppy from a reputable breeder will definitely pay off in the long run. Look for a dedicated and ethical breeder who values good health and stable personalities, and who really cares what happens to the dog for the rest of his life.

it's a Fact

Local breeder referrals are essential. A breeder who belongs to a Siberian Husky club demonstrates active involvement in the breed, and breeds according to that particular club's code of ethics. That's who you want to do business with: a breeder who abides by a code of ethics.

Why is this so important? This breed has a unique personality who needs to be bred correctly by someone with experience who really knows what he or she is doing. If not, you may wind up with a dog who's overly aggressive, has a ton of health problems and doesn't even look like the Siberian Husky.

Avoid puppy mills and backyard breeders. Puppy mills are large-scale breeding operations that produce puppies in an assembly-line fashion without regard to health and socialization. Backyard breeders, on the other hand, can be well-meaning, regular husky owners who simply do not possess enough knowledge about the Siberian Husky breed and breeding to produce healthy puppies.

The American Kennel Club and the United Kennel Club provide a list of breeders in good standing with their organizations. Visit their websites, listed in the Resources chapter on page 166, for more information.

EVALUATING BREEDERS

Once you have the names and numbers of breeders in your area, start contacting them to find out more about their breeding programs. But, before you contact them, prepare some questions to ask that will get you the information you need to know.

Did You Know?

Good Breeder Signs
When you visit a Siberian Husky breeder, look around the dwelling for:
- a clean, well-maintained facility
- no overwhelming odors
- an overall impression of cleanliness
- socialized dogs and puppies

Prospective buyers interview breeders in much the same way that a breeder should interview a buyer. Make a list of questions, record the answers and compare them to the answers from other breeders whom you may interview later. The right questions are those that help you identify who has been in the breed a respectable number of years and who is actively showing their dogs. Ask in-depth questions regarding the genetic health of the parents, grandparents and great grandparents of any puppy you are considering. Ask what sort of genetic testing program the breeder adheres to.

You should look to see if a breeder actively shows his or her dogs in conformation events (aka dog shows). Showing indicates that the breeder is bringing out examples from his or her breeding program for the public to see. If there are obvious problems, such as temperament or general conformation, they will be readily apparent. Also, the main reason to breed Siberian Huskies is to improve the quality of the breed. If the breeder is not showing, then he or she is more likely to be breeding purely for the monetary aspect and may have less concern for the welfare and future of the breed.

Inquiring about health and determining the breeder's willingness to work with you in the future are also important for the potential puppy buyer to learn. The prospective buyer should see what kind of health guarantees the breeder gives. You should also find out if the breeder will be available for future consultation regarding your Siberian Husky, and find out if the breeder will take your dog back if something unforeseen happens.

Prospective buyers should ask plenty of questions, and in return, buyers should also be prepared to answer questions posed by a responsible breeder who wants to make sure

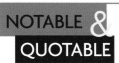

Siberians are very independent, so as a trainer, you need to be confident and believe in your ability to train your dog, as well as be consistent in what you expect from them. — Theresa Przybylski, chairperson of the obedience, rally and agility committee of the Siberian Husky Club of America, from Crete, Ill.

his or her puppy is going to a good home. Be prepared for a battery of questions from the breeder regarding your purpose for wanting this breed of dog and whether you can properly care for one. Avoid buying from a breeder who does little or no screening. If a breeder doesn't ask any questions, they are not concerned with where their pups end up. In this case, the dogs' best interests are probably not the breeder's motive for breeding.

The buyer should find a breeder who is willing to answer any questions they have and is knowledgeable about the history of the breed, health issues and about the background of their own dogs. Learn about a breeder's long-term commitment to the Siberian Husky breed and to his or her puppies after they leave the kennel.

Look for breeders who know their purpose for producing a particular litter, those who are knowledgeable in the pedigrees of their dogs and of the Siberian Husky breed itself, and have had the necessary health screenings performed on the parents. They should also ask you for references to show that they are interested in establishing a relationship with you in consideration for a puppy. If after one phone conversation with a breeder, the person is supplying you with an address in which to send a deposit, continue your search for a reputable husky breeder elsewhere.

CHOOSING THE RIGHT PUP

Once you have found a breeder you are comfortable with, your next step is to pick the right puppy. The good news is that if you have done your homework and found a responsible breeder, you can count on this person to give you plenty of help in choosing the right pup for your personality and lifestyle. In fact, most good breeders will recommend a specific puppy once they know what kind of dog you want.

After you have narrowed down the search and selected a reputable breeder, rely on the experience of the breeder to help you select your puppy. The selection of the puppy depends a lot on what purpose the pup is being purchased for. If the pup is being purchased as a show prospect, the breeder will offer his or her assessment of the pups that meet this criteria and be able to explain the strengths and faults of each pup.

Whether you are looking for a show- or a pet-quality husky, a good, stable temperament is vital for a happy relationship. Generally, you want to avoid a timid puppy or a very dominant one. Temperament is very important, and a reputable breeder should spend a lot of time with the pups and be able to offer an evaluation of each pup's personality.

A reputable breeder probably will tell you which Siberian Husky puppy is appropriate for your home situation and personality. They may not allow you to choose the puppy, although they certainly will take your preference into consideration.

Some breeders, on the other hand, believe it's important for you to be heavily

Did You Know? Healthy puppies have clear eyes and shiny coats, and are playful and friendly. An important factor in a puppy's long-term health and good temperament is the age she goes to her permanent home, which should be between 8 and 10 weeks. This gives the pups plenty of time to develop immunity and bond with their mom.

Questions to Expect
Be prepared for the breeder to ask you some questions, too.

1. Have you previously owned a Siberian Husky?

The breeder is trying to gauge how familiar you are with the breed. If you have never owned one, illustrate your knowledge of Siberian Huskies by telling the breeder about your research.

2. Do you have children? What are their ages?

Some breeders are wary about selling a dog to families with younger chil-

dren. This isn't a steadfast rule, and some breeders only insist on meeting the kids to see how they handle puppies. It all depends on the breeder.

3. How long have you wanted a Siberian Husky?

This helps a breeder know if this purchase is an impulse buy or a carefully thought-out decision. Buying on impulse is one of the biggest mistakes owners can make. Be patient.

Join Club Husky to get a complete list of questions a breeder should ask you. Click on "Downloads" at:
DogChannel.com/Club-Husky

involved in selecting the puppy. They will let you make the decision on which pup to take home because not everyone is looking for the same things in a dog. Some people want a quiet, laidback attitude. Others want an outgoing, active dog. When pups are old enough to go to their new homes at roughly 8 to 10 weeks of age, these breeders prefer you make your own decision because no one can tell at this age which pup will make the most intelligent or affectionate dog. The color, sex and markings are obvious, but that is about all you can tell for sure at this age. Everything else being equal — size, health, etc. — some breeders suggest picking the pup whom you have a gut feeling for.

By selecting a puppy from a responsible breeder, you will eliminate many health issues.

The chemistry between a buyer and puppy is important and should play a role in determining which pup goes to which home. When possible, make numerous visits to see the puppies, and in effect, let a puppy choose you. There usually will be one puppy who spends more time with a buyer and is more comfortable relaxing and sitting with, or on, a person.

CHECKING FOR HUSKY QUALITIES

Whether you are dealing with a breeder who wants to pick a puppy for you or who lets you make the decision alone, consider certain points when evaluating the Siberian puppy who you may end up calling your own. The puppy should be friendly and outgoing, not skittish in any way. He should be forgiving of correction. He shouldn't be too terribly mouthy. The pup should readily follow you and be willing to snuggle in your lap and be turned onto his back easily without a problem.

Proper temperament is very important. A Siberian Husky puppy who has a dominant personality requires an experienced owner who will be firm during training. A puppy who is a little shy requires heavy socialization to build his confidence.

You also can evaluate a Siberian Husky puppy's temperament on your own. The temperament of the pups can be evaluated by spending some time watching them. If you can visit the pups and observe them together with their littermates, then you can see how they interact with each other. You may be able to pinpoint which ones are the bullies and which ones are more submissive. In general, look for a puppy who is more interested in you than in his littermates. Then, take each pup individually to a new location away from the rest of the litter. Put the puppy down on the

With the popularity of Siberian Huskies, shelters and rescue groups across the country are often inundated with sweet, loving examples of the breed — from the tiniest puppies to senior dogs,

petite females to strapping males. Often, to get the husky of your dreams, it takes a trip to the local shelter. Or, perhaps you could find your ideal dog waiting patiently in the arms of a foster parent at a nearby rescue group. It just takes a bit of effort, patience and a willingness to find the right dog for your family, not just the cutest dog on the block.

The perks of owning a Siberian Husky are plentiful: companionship, unconditional love, true loyalty and laughter, just to name a few. So why choose the adoption option? Because you literally will be saving a life!

Owners of adopted dogs swear they're more grateful and loving than any dog they've owned before. It's almost as if they knew what dire fate awaited them and are so thankful to you. Siberian Huskies, known for their people-pleasing personalities, seem to embody this mentality wholeheartedly when they're rescued. And they want to give something back. Another perk: Almost all adopted dogs come fully vetted, with proper medical treat-

ment, vaccinations and medicine, as well as being spayed or neutered. Some are even licensed and microchipped.

Don't disregard older dogs, thinking the only good pair-up is between you and a puppy. Adult Siberian Huskies are more established behaviorally and personality-wise, helping to better mesh their characteristics with yours in this game of matchmaker. Puppies are always in high demand, so if you open your options to include adults, you will have a better chance of adopting quickly. Plus, adult dogs are often housetrained, more calm, chew-proof and don't need to be taken outside in the middle of the night ... five times ... in the pouring rain.

The Siberian Husky Club of America offers rescue support information or log onto Petfinder.com. The site's searchable database enables you to find a Siberian Husky in your area who needs a break in the form of a compassionate owner like you. More websites are listed in the Resources chapter on page 166.

ground, walk away and see how he reacts away from the security of his littermates. The pup may be afraid at first, but he should gradually recover and start checking out the new surroundings.

D-I-Y TEMPERAMENT TEST

Puppies come in a wide assortment of temperaments to suit almost everyone. If you are looking for a dog who is easily trainable and a good companion to your family, you most likely want a puppy with a medium temperament.

Temperament testing can help you determine the type of disposition your potential puppy possesses. A pup with a medium temperament will have the following reactions to these various tests, best conducted when the pup is 7 weeks old.

Step 1. To test a pup's social attraction and his confidence in approaching humans, coax him toward you by kneeling down and clapping your hands gently. A pup with a medium temperament comes readily, tail up or down.

Step 2. To test a husky pup's eagerness to follow, walk away from him while he is watching you. He should follow you readily, tail up.

Step 3. To see how a pup handles restraint, kneel down and roll the pup gently on his back. Using a light but firm touch, hold him in this position with one hand for 30 seconds. The Siberian Husky pup should settle down after some initial struggle at first and offer some or steady eye contact.

Step 4. To evaluate a puppy's level of social dominance, stand up, then crouch down beside the pup and stroke him from head to back. A Siberian Husky puppy with a medium temperament — neither too dominant nor too submissive — should cuddle up to you and lick your face, or squirm and lick your hands.

Step 5. An additional test of a pup's dominance level is to bend over, cradle the pup under his belly with your fingers interlaced and palms up, and elevate him just off the ground. Hold him there for 30 seconds. The pup should not struggle and should be relaxed, or he should struggle and then settle down and lick you.

PHYSICAL FEATURES

To assess a puppy's health, take a deliberate, thorough look at each part of his body. Signs of a healthy puppy include bright eyes, a healthy coat, a good appetite and firm stool. Watch for a telltale link between physical and mental health. A healthy Siberian Husky, as with any breed of puppy, will display a happier, more positive attitude than an unhealthy puppy. A Siberian Husky puppy's belly should not be over extended or hard, as this may be a sign of worms. Also, if you are around the litter long enough to witness a bowel movement, the stool should be solid, and the pup should not show any signs of discomfort. Look into the pup's eyes, too; they should be bright and full of life.

Breeder Q&A

Here are some questions you should ask a breeder and the answers you want.

Q. How often do you have litters available?

A. You want to hear "once or twice a year" or "occasionally" because a breeder who doesn't have litters that often is probably more concerned with the quality of his puppies, rather than with making money.

Q. What kinds of health problems do huskies have?

A. Beware of a breeder who says "none." Every breed has health issues. For Siberian Huskies, some genetic health problems include hip dysplasia, cataracts and progressive retinal atrophy.

Get a complete list of questions to ask a Siberian Husky breeder — and the ideal answers — at Club Husky. Log onto **DogChannel.com/Club-Husky** and click on "Downloads."

When purchasing a Siberian puppy, buyers hear from breeders that these dogs are just like any other puppy — times 10! They are very smart, stubborn and often have their own agendas. If a prospective owner isn't willing to spend a fair amount of time with a Siberian Husky, then the breed is not for them. A Siberian Husky wants to be with people more than other dogs and is quite similar to a 7-year-old boy in the sense that he needs attention and consistent reinforcement for behavioral parameters. Once through adolescence, however, a Siberian Husky is the best friend, guardian and companion a person or family could have.

PUPPY PARTICULARS

Here are signs to look for when picking a puppy from a breeder. When in doubt, ask the breeder which puppy they think has the best personality/temperament to fit your lifestyle.

1. Look at the area where the puppies spend most of their time. It's OK if they play outdoors part of the day, but they should sleep indoors at night so they can interact with people and become accustomed to hearing ordinary household noises, such as a vacuum cleaner or a washing machine. This builds a solid foundation for a well-socialized and secure Siberian Husky puppy. The puppies' area should be clean, well lit, have fresh drinking water and interesting toys.

2. Sure, you're only buying one puppy, but make sure to see all of the puppies in the litter. By 5 weeks of age, healthy pups will begin playing with one another and should be lively and energetic. It's OK if they're asleep when you visit, but stay long enough to see them wake up. Once they're up, they shouldn't be lethargic or weak, as this may be a sign of illness.

3. Puppies should be confident and eager to greet you. A Siberian Husky pup who is shy or fearful and stays in the corner may be sick or insecure. Although some introverted pups come out of their shells later on, many do not. These dogs will always be fearful as adults and are not good choices for an active, noisy family with or without children, or for people who have never had a dog before. These shy pups frighten easily and will require a tremendous amount of training and socialization in order to live a happy life.

Choose a pup who is happy and eager to interact with you but reject the one who is either too shy or too bossy. These temperament types are a challenge to deal with, and require a tremendous amount of training to socialize. The perfect Siberian Husky puppy personality is somewhere between the two extremes.

4. If it's feeding time during your visit, all pups should be eager to gobble up their food. A puppy who refuses to eat may signal illness.

5. The dog's skin should be smooth, clean and shiny without any sores or

> it's a **Fact**
>
> Food intolerance is the inability of the dog to completely digest certain foods. Puppies who may have done very well on their mother's milk may not do well on cow's milk. The result of this food intolerance may be loose bowels, passing gas and stomach pains. These are the only obvious symptoms of food intolerance, which makes diagnosis difficult.

bumps. Puppies should not be biting or scratching at themselves continuously, as this could signal fleas.

6. After 10 to 12 days, the puppies' eyes should be open and clear without any redness or discharges. Pups should not be scratching at their eyes, as this may cause an infection or signal irritation.

7. Vomiting or coughing more than once is not normal. If this occurs, a Siberian Husky pup might be ill and should visit the veterinarian immediately.

8. Visit long enough to see the puppies eliminate. All stools should be firm without being watery or bloody. These are signs of illness or that a puppy has worms.

9. Siberian Husky puppies should walk or run freely without limping.

10. A healthy Siberian Husky puppy who is getting enough to eat should not be skinny. You should be able to slightly feel his ribs if you rub his abdomen, but you should not be able to see the ribs protruding.

BREEDER PAPERS

Everything today comes with its own instruction manual. When you purchase a Siberian Husky puppy, it's no different. A reputable breeder should give you a registration application; a sales contract; a health guarantee; your puppy's complete health records; a three-, four- or five-generation pedigree; and some general information on Siberian Husky behavior, care, conformation, health and training.

Registration Application. This document from the AKC or UKC assigns your puppy a number and identifies the dog by listing his date of birth, the names of the parents and shows that he is registered as a purebred Siberian Husky. It doesn't prove whether or not your dog is a show- or a pet-quality Siberian Husky and doesn't provide any health guarantee.

Sales Contract. A reputable breeder should discuss the terms of the contract with you before asking you to sign it. This is a written understanding of both of your expectations and shows that the breeder cares about the pup's welfare throughout their life. The contract can include such terms as requiring you to keep your dog indoors at night, spaying or neutering if your puppy is not going to be a show dog, providing routine vet care and assurance that you'll feed your dog a healthy diet. Most responsible breeders will ask that you take your dog to obedience classes and earn a Canine Good Citizen title (an AKC training certification for dogs that exhibit good manners) before he is 2 years old. Many breeders also require new owners to have totally secure fencing and gates around their yard. Siberian Huskies are incredible escape artists, and they will find a way out of the yard if there's even the slightest opening available.

Health Guarantee. This includes a letter from a veterinarian that the puppy has been examined and is healthy, and states that the breeder will replace your dog if he were to develop a genetic, life-threatening illness during his lifetime.

Health Records. Here's everything you want to know about your puppy's, and his parents', health. It should include the dates your puppy was vaccinated, dewormed and examined by a veterinarian for signs of heart murmur, plus the parents' test results for the presence or absence of hip and elbow dysplasia, heart problems and luxated patellas.

Pedigree. Breeders should provide you with a copy of the puppy's three-, four- or five-generation pedigree. Many breeders also have photos of the dog's ancestors that they will proudly share with you.

Extra Information. The best Siberian Husky breeders pride themselves on handing over to a new owner a notebook full of the latest information on Siberian Husky behavior, care, conformation, health and training. Be sure to read it because it will provide valuable help while raising your Siberian Husky.

Healthy Puppy Signs

Here are a few things you should look for when selecting a puppy from a litter.

1. **NOSE:** It should be slightly moist to the touch, but there shouldn't be excessive discharge. The puppy should not be sneezing or sniffling persistently.

2. **SKIN AND COAT:** Your husky puppy's coat should be soft and shiny, without flakes or excessive shedding. Watch out for patches of missing hair, redness, bumps or sores. The pup should have a pleasant smell. Check for parasites, such as fleas or ticks.

3. **BEHAVIOR:** A healthy Siberian Husky puppy may be sleepy, but he should not be lethargic. A healthy puppy will be playful at times, not isolated in a corner. You should see occasional bursts of energy and interaction with his littermates. When it's mealtime, a healthy puppy will take an interest in his food.

There are more signs to look for when picking out the perfect husky puppy for your lifestyle. Download the list at **DogChannel.com/Club-Husky**

A healthy Siberian Husky puppy will be curious, playful and interested in you.

ESSENTIALS

Don't for one second think that a Siberian Husky would prefer to live outside on the frozen tundra of Siberia! He, like every other breed, wants to live in the best accommodations with plenty of toys, soft bedding and other luxuries. Your home is now his home, too; and, before you even bring that new puppy or rescue dog into his new forever home, be a smart owner and make your home accessible for him.

In fact, in order for him to grow into a stable, well-adjusted dog, he has to feel comfortable in his surroundings. Remember, he is leaving the warmth and security of his mother and littermates, as well as the familiarity of the only place he has ever known, so it is important to make his transition to your home — his new home — as easy as possible.

Aside from making sure that your Siberian Husky will be comfortable in your home, you also have to ensure that your home is safe, which means taking the proper precautions to keep your puppy away from things that are dangerous for him. Just like when bringing a new baby home, you must prepare.

it's a
Fact

Dangers lurk indoors and outdoors. Keep your curious Siberian Husky from investigating your shed and garage. Antifreeze and fertilizers, such as those you would use for roses, can kill any dog. Keep these items on high shelves that are out of reach.

A well-stocked toy box should contain three main categories of toys.

1. **action** — anything that you can throw or roll and get things moving
2. **distraction** — durable toys that make dogs work for a treat
3. **comfort** — soft, stuffed "security blankets"

PUPPY-PROOF

Puppy-proof your home inside and out before bringing your Siberian Husky home for the first time. Place breakables out of reach. If he is limited to certain places within the house, keep potentially dangerous items in off-limit areas. If your Siberian Husky is going to spend time in a crate, make sure that there isn't anything near it that he can reach if he sticks his curious little nose or paws through the openings.

The outside of your home must also be safe. Your pup will want to run and explore the yard, and he should be granted that freedom — as long as you are there to supervise. Do not let a fence give you a false sense of security; you would be surprised how crafty and persistent a Siberian Husky puppy can be in figuring out how to dig under a fence or squeeze his way through holes. The remedy is to make the fence well embedded into the ground. Be sure to repair or secure any gaps in the fence. Check the fence periodically to ensure that it is in good shape and make repairs as needed; a very determined puppy may work on the same spot until he is able to get through.

The following are a few common problem areas to watch out for in the home.

■ **Electrical cords and wiring:** No electrical cord or wiring is safe. Many office-supply stores sell products to keep wires gathered under computer desks, as well as products that prevent office chair wheels (and puppy teeth) from damaging electrical cords. If you have exposed cords and wires, these products aren't very expensive and can be used to keep a puppy out of trouble.

■ **Trash cans:** Don't waste your time trying to train your Siberian Husky not to get into the trash. Simply put the garbage behind a cabinet door and use a child-safe lock, if necessary. Dogs love bathroom trash, which consists of items that can be extremely dangerous (i.e., cotton balls, cotton swabs, used razors, dental floss, etc.)! Put the bathroom trash can in a cabinet and make sure you always shut the door to the bathroom.

■ **Household cleaners:** Make sure your Siberian Husky puppy doesn't have access to any of these deadly chemicals. Keep them behind closed cabinet doors, using child-safe locks, if necessary.

■ **Pest control sprays and poisons:** Chemicals to control ants or other pests should never be used in the house, if possible. Your Siberian Husky pup doesn't have to directly ingest these poisons to become ill; if he steps in the poison, he can experience toxic effects by licking his paws. Roach motels and other toxic pest traps are also yummy to dogs, so don't drop these behind couches or cabinets; if there's room for a roach motel, there's room for a determined Siberian Husky.

■ **Fabric:** Here's one you might not think about: Some puppies have a habit of licking blankets, upholstery, rugs or carpets. Though this habit seems fairly innocuous, over time the fibers from the upholstery or carpet can accumulate in the

Puppies need toys to chew on to relieve teething pain and pressure, as well as just to have fun.

dog's stomach and cause a blockage. If you see your dog licking these items, remove the item or prevent him from having contact with it.

■ **Prescriptions, painkillers, supplements and vitamins:** Keep all medications in a cabinet. Also, be very careful when taking your prescription medications, supplements or vitamins: How often have you dropped a pill? You can be sure that your Siberian Husky puppy will be in between your legs and will snarf up the pill before you even start to say "No!" Dispense your own pills carefully and without your Siberian Husky present.

■ **Miscellaneous loose items:** If it's not bolted to the floor, your puppy is likely to give the item a taste test. Socks, coins, children's toys, game pieces, cat toys — you name it. If it's on the floor, it's worth a try. Make sure the floors in your home are picked up and free of clutter.

FAMILY INTRODUCTIONS

Everyone in the house will be excited about the puppy's homecoming and will want to pet and play with him, but it is best to make the introduction low-key so as not to overwhelm your puppy. He will already be apprehensive. It is the first time he has been separated from his mother, littermates and breeder, and the ride to your home is likely to be the first time he has been in a car. The last thing you want to do is smother your Siberian Husky pup, as this will only frighten him further. This is not to

Before you bring your Siberian Husky home, make sure you don't have anything that can put her in harm's way. Go to Club Husky and download a list of poisonous plants and foods to avoid. Log on to **DogChannel.com/Club-Husky** and click on "Downloads."

say that human contact is unnecessary at this stage because this is the time when a connection between the pup and his human family is formed. Gentle petting and soothing words should help console your Siberian Husky, as well as letting him down to explore on his own (under your watchful eye, of course).

Your pup may approach the family members, or may busy himself with exploring the house or yard for a while. Gradually, each person should spend some time with the puppy, one at a time, crouching down to get as close to his level as possible, letting him sniff their hands before petting him gently. He definitely needs human attention, and he needs to be touched; this is how to form an immediate bond. Just remember that the pup is experiencing a lot of things for the first time, all at once.

There are new people, new noises, new smells and new things to investigate. Be gentle, be affectionate and be as comforting as you can possibly be.

PUP'S FIRST NIGHT HOME

You have traveled home with your new puppy safely in his crate. He may have already been to the vet for a thorough check-up — he's been weighed, his papers exam-

SMART TIP!

When you are unable to watch your Siberian Husky puppy, put her in a crate or an exercise pen on an easily cleanable floor. If she has an accident on carpeting, clean it completely and meticulously, so that it doesn't smell like her potty forever.

Don't overwhelm your puppy on his first night home with too many people or too many toys.

9-1-1! If you don't know whether the plant, food or "stuff" your Siberian Husky just ate is toxic to dogs, call the ASPCA's Animal Poison Control Center (888-426-4435). Be prepared to provide your puppy's age and weight, her symptoms — if any — and how much of the plant, chemical, or substance she ingested, as well as how long ago you think she came into contact with the substance. The ASPCA charges a consultation fee for this service.

ined, perhaps he's even been vaccinated and dewormed as well. Your Siberian Husky has met and licked the whole family, including the excited children and the less-than-happy cat. He's explored his area, his new bed, the yard and everywhere else he's permitted. He's eaten his first meal at home and relieved himself in the proper place. Your Siberian Husky has heard lots of new sounds, smelled new friends and seen more of the outside world than ever before. This was just the first day! He's worn out and is ready for bed — or so you think!

Remember, this is your puppy's first night to sleep alone. His mother and littermates are no longer at paw's length, and he's scared, cold and lonely. Be reassuring to your new family member. This is not the time to spoil your Siberian Husky and give in to his inevitable whining.

Puppies whine. They whine to let others know where they are and hopefully to get company out of it. Place your Siberian Husky puppy in his new bed or crate in his room and close the door. Mercifully, he may fall asleep without a peep. If the inevitable

occurs, ignore the whining; he is fine. Do not give in and visit your Siberian Husky puppy; he will fall asleep eventually.

Many breeders recommend placing a piece of bedding from his former home in his new bed so that he will recognize the scent of his littermates. Others still advise placing a hot water bottle in his bed for warmth. The latter may be a good idea provided the pup doesn't attempt to suckle.

Your Siberian Husky's first night can be somewhat terrifying for him. Remember that you set the tone of nighttime at your house. Unless you want to play with your pup every night at 10 p.m., midnight and 2 a.m., don't initiate the habit. Your family will thank you, and so will your pup!

PET-SUPPLY STORE SHOPPING

It's fun shopping for new things for a new puppy. From training to feeding and sleeping to playing, your new pup will need a few items to make life comfy, easy and fun. Be prepared and visit a pet-supply store before you bring home your new family member.

◆ **Collar and ID tag:** Accustom your dog to wearing a collar the first day you bring him home. Not only will a collar and ID tag help your puppy in the event that he becomes lost, but collars are also an important training tool. If your Siberian Husky gets into trouble, the collar will act as a handle, helping you divert him to a more appropriate behavior. Make sure the collar fits snugly enough so that your husky cannot wriggle out of it, but is loose enough so that it will not be uncomfortably tight around his neck. You should be able to fit a finger between your pup's neck and the collar. Collars come in many styles, but for starting out, a simple buckle collar with an easy-release snap works great.

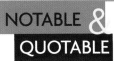
Playing with toys from puppyhood encourages good behavior and social skills throughout your dog's life. A happy, playful dog is a content and well-adjusted one. Also, because all puppies chew to soothe their gums and help loosen puppy teeth, dogs should always have easy access to several different toys.

— dog trainer and author Harrison Forbes of Savannah, Tenn.

SMART TIP!

Keep a crate in your vehicle and take your Siberian along when you visit the drive-thru at the bank or your favorite fast-food restaurant. She can watch interactions, hear interesting sounds and maybe earn a dog treat.

◆ **Leash:** For training or just for taking a stroll down the street, a leash is your Siberian Husky's vehicle to explore the outside world. Like collars, leashes come in a variety of styles and materials. A 6-foot nylon leash is a popular choice because it is lightweight and durable. As your pup grows and gets used to walking on the leash, you may want to purchase a flexible leash. These leads allow you to extend the length to give your dog a broader area to explore or to shorten the length to keep your dog closer to you.

◆ **Bowls:** Your Siberian Husky will need two bowls: one for water and one for food. You may want two sets of bowls, one for inside and one for outside, depending on where your dog will be fed and where he will be spending time. Bowls should be sturdy enough so that they don't tip over easily. (Most have reinforced bottoms that prevent tipping.) Bowls usually are made of metal, ceramic or plastic, and should be easy to clean.

◆ **Crate:** A multipurpose crate serves as a bed, housetraining tool and travel carrier. It also is the ideal doggie den — a bedroom of sorts — that your Siberian Husky can retire to when he wants to rest or just needs a break.

The crate should be large enough for your dog to stand, turn around and lie down. You don't want any more room than this — especially if you're planning on using the crate to housetrain your dog — because he will eliminate in one corner and lie down in another. Get a crate that is big enough for your dog when he is an adult. Then, use dividers to limit the space when he's a puppy.

◆ **Bed:** A plush doggie bed will make sleeping and resting more comfortable for your Siberian Husky. Dog beds come in all shapes, sizes and colors, but your dog just needs one that is soft and large enough for him to stretch out on. Because puppies and rescue dogs may not always be house-

The first thing you should always do before your puppy comes home is to lie on the ground and look around. You want to be able to see everything your puppy is going to see. For the puppy, the world is one big chew toy.

— *Cathleen Stamm, rescue volunteer in San Diego, Calif.*

trained, it's helpful to buy a bed that can be easily washed. If your Siberian Husky will be sleeping in a crate, a nice crate pad and a small blanket that he can "burrow" in will help him feel more at home. Replace the blanket if it becomes ragged and starts to fall apart because your Siberian Husky's nails could get caught in it.

◆ **Gate:** Similar to those used for toddlers, gates help keep your Siberian Husky confined to one room or area when you can't supervise him. Gates also work to keep your dog out of areas you don't want him in, and they are available in many styles. Make sure you choose one with openings small enough so your puppy can't squeeze through the bars or any gaps.

◆ **Cleaning supplies:** Until your Siberian Husky puppy is housetrained, you will be doing a lot of cleaning. Accidents will occur, which is acceptable in the beginning because the puppy doesn't know any better. All you can do is be pre-

pared to clean up any accidents. Old rags, towels, newspapers and a stain-and-odor remover are good to have on hand.

◆ **Toys:** Today, your canine toy selection is almost unlimited. There are chew toys, stuffed toys, rubber toys, squeaky toys and interactive toys.

For teething puppies, chew toys provide a gum-soothing workout that helps keep those sharp teeth off your coffee table. Types vary from those chewed away in one or two sittings to others that last weeks or

months. Though both are beneficial, as your husky grows and his jaw strength increases, edible chew toys sometimes become barely more than a snack.

Most puppies love soft, stuffed toys, sometimes choosing a favorite to carry around and cuddle. Other puppies love tearing these toys apart! A smart owner will be mindful of the danger that the puppy might ingest parts of the stuffing or fabric and suffer an internal blockage.

Rubber toys present a sturdy yet soft option that many puppies enjoy chewing, chasing and fetching. Unless you own a Siberian Husky puppy with particularly strong jaws, quality rubber toys can usually be left safely with your husky. Note: Never give your puppy a rubber toy small enough for him to swallow. The slippery surface slides down far too easily and makes it impossible to remove.

Squeaky toys come in countless shapes, forms and materials. Often useful as a training motivator, these toys have a major drawback. Many puppies and dogs become obsessed about "killing" the squeaker and often succeed by ripping the toy apart. The danger is that your husky could swallow the ripped pieces, causing a choking hazard or a potential intestinal blockage. Be sure to always supervise your dog's playtime with these toys.

Innovative and invaluable when raising a lively puppy, interactive toys help to keep your dog busy, develop his mind and burn off energy. With most interactive toys, your puppy extracts treats by licking them out, rolling the toy or playing with it. This self-reward system maintains interest until the goodies are gone.

Your husky might also like to chase and catch balls that roll and bounce. The kind of balls you should buy will depend on you and

Funny Bone

To err is human; to forgive, canine.

— *Anonymous*

your dog's preferences. Just keep in mind that many dogs die each year from choking on a ball. Replace them as your husky grows, so that they'll always be the appropriate size for his mouth and throat.

BEYOND THE BASICS

The basic items discussed previously are the bare necessities. You will find out what else you and your new dog need as you go along — grooming supplies, flea/tick protection — and these things will vary depending on your situation. It is important, however, that you have everything you need to make your Siberian Husky comfortable in his new home.

**Some ordinary household items make great toys for your husky —
as long you make sure they are safe.** Tennis balls, plastic water
bottles, old towels and more can be transformed into fun with
a little creativity. You can find a list of homemade toys at
DogChannel.com/Club-Husky

HOUSETRAINING

Unexciting as it may be, the housetraining part of puppy rearing greatly affects the budding relationship between a smart owner and his puppy — particularly when it becomes an area of ongoing contention. Fortunately, armed with suitable knowledge, patience and common sense, you'll find housetraining progresses at a relatively smooth rate. That leaves more time for the important things, like cuddling your adorable puppy, showing him off and laughing at his high jinks.

The answer to successful housetraining is total supervision and management. Crates, tethers, exercise pens and leashes should be used until you know your dog has developed preferences for outside surfaces (grass, gravel, concrete) instead of carpet, tile or hardwood. Then, he'll know that potty happens outside.

IN THE BEGINNING

For the first two to three weeks of a puppy's life, his mother helps the pup to eliminate. The mother also keeps the whelping box or "nest area" clean. When pups begin to walk around and eat on their

it's a Fact

Ongoing housetraining difficulties may indicate your puppy has a health problem, warranting a vet check. A urinary infection, parasites, a virus and other nasty issues greatly affect your puppy's ability to hold pee or poop.

own, they choose where they eliminate. You can train your puppy to relieve himself wherever you choose, but this must be somewhere suitable. You should keep in mind from the outset that when your puppy is old enough to go out in public places, you must be considerate and pick up after him. You will always have to carry with you a small plastic bag or poop scoop.

Outdoor training includes such surfaces as grass, soil and concrete. Indoor training usually means training your dog on newspaper. When deciding on the surface and location that you want your Siberian Husky to use, be sure it is going to be permanent. Training your dog on grass and then changing to gravel two months later is extremely difficult him, as well as you.

Next, choose the cue you will use each and every time you want your puppy to eliminate. "Let's go," "hurry up" and "potty" are examples of cues commonly used by smart dog owners.

Get in the habit of giving your puppy the chosen relief cue before you take him out. That way, when he becomes an adult, you will be able to determine if he wants to go out when you ask him. A confirmation will be signs of interest, such as wagging his tail, watching you intently or going to the door.

LET'S START WITH THE CRATE

Clean animals by nature, dogs dislike soiling where they sleep and eat. This fact makes a crate a useful tool for housetraining. When purchasing a new crate, consider that an appropriately sized crate will allow adequate room for an adult dog to stand full-height, lie on his side without scrunching and turn around easily. If debating plastic versus wire crates, short-haired breeds sometimes prefer the warmer, draft-blocking quality of plastic, while furry dogs often like the cooling airflow of a wire crate.

Some crates come with a movable wall that reduces the interior size to provide enough space for your puppy to stand, turn and lie down, while not allowing him room to soil one end and sleep in the other. The problem is that if your puppy goes potty in the crate anyway, the divider forces him to lie in his own excrement.

A properly sized crate is key to
successful housetraining.

This can work against you by desensitizing your puppy against his normal, instinctive revulsion to resting where he has just eliminated. If scheduling permits you or a responsible family member to clean the crate soon after it's soiled, then you can continue to cratetrain because limiting crate size does encourage your puppy to hold it. Otherwise, give him enough room to move away from an unclean area until he's better able to control his elimination.

Needless to say, not every Siberian Husky puppy advances at the same rate. If your Siberian Husky moves along at a faster pace, thank your lucky stars. Should he progress slower, accept it and remind yourself that he'll improve. Be aware that puppies frequently hold it longer at night than during the day. Just because your puppy sleeps for six or more hours through the night does not mean he can hold it that long during the more active daytime hours.

One last bit of crate advice: Place it in the corner of a high-traffic room, such as the family room or kitchen. Social and curious by nature, dogs like to feel included in family happenings. Creating a quiet retreat by putting the crate in an unused area may seem like a good idea, but results in your puppy feeling insecure and isolated. Watching his people pop in and out of the crate room reassures your puppy that he's not forgotten.

A PUP'S GOT NEEDS

Your puppy needs to relieve himself after play periods, after each meal, after he has been sleeping and any time he indicates that he is looking for a place to urinate or defecate.

The urinary and intestinal tract muscles of very young puppies are not fully developed. Therefore, like human babies, puppies need to relieve themselves frequently. Take your puppy out often — every hour for an 8-week-old, for example — and always immediately after sleeping and eating. The older the puppy, the less often he will need to relieve himself. Finally, as a mature, healthy adult, he will require only three to five relief trips per day.

How often does a Siberian Husky puppy do his business? A lot! Go to **DogChannel.com/Club-Husky** and download the typical peeing and pooping schedule of a puppy. You can also download a chart that you can fill out to track your dog's elimination timetable, which will help you with housetraining.

Reward your pup with a high-value treat immediately after he potties to reinforce going in the proper location, then play for a short time afterward. This teaches that good things happen after pottying outside! — Victoria Schade, certified pet dog trainer, from Annandale, Va.

If you acquire your Siberian Husky puppy at 8 weeks of age, expect to take her out at least six to eight times a day. By the time she's about 6 months old, potty trips will be down to three or four times a day. A rule of thumb is to take your puppy out in hourly intervals equal to her age in months.

HOUSING HELPS

Because the types of housing and control you provide for your Siberian Husky puppy have a direct relationship on the success of housetraining, you must consider the various aspects of both before beginning training. Taking a new puppy home and turning him loose in your house can be compared to turning a child loose in a sports arena and telling the child that the place is all his! The sheer enormity of the place would be too much for him to handle. Instead, offer the puppy clearly defined areas where he can play, sleep, eat and live. A room of the house where the family gathers is the most obvious choice.

Puppies are social animals and need to feel like they are a part of the pack right from the start. Hearing your voice, watching you while you are doing things and smelling you nearby are all positive reinforcers that he is now a member of your pack. Usually a family room, the kitchen or a nearby adjoining breakfast area is ideal for providing safety and security for puppy and owner.

Within that room, there should be a smaller area that your Siberian Husky puppy can call his own. An alcove, a wire or fiberglass dog crate, or a fenced (not boarded!) corner from which he can view the activities of his new family will be fine. The designated area should be lined with clean bedding and a toy. Water must always be available, in a nonspill container, once your dog is housetrained.

IN CONTROL

By control, we mean helping your puppy to create a lifestyle pattern that will be compatible to that of his human pack (you!). Just as we guide children to learn our way of life, we must show our Siberian Husky pup when it is time to play, eat, sleep, exercise and entertain himself.

Your puppy should always sleep in his crate. He should also learn that, during times of household confusion and excessive human activity, such as at breakfast when family members are preparing for the day, he can play by himself in relative safety and comfort in his designated area. Each time you leave your Siberian Husky alone, he should understand exactly where he is supposed to stay.

Other times of excitement, such as family parties, can be fun for your puppy, provided that he can view the activities from the security of his designated area. He is not underfoot, and he is not being fed all sorts of tidbits that will probably cause him stomach distress, yet he still feels a part of the fun.

Puppies are chewers. They cannot tell the difference between lamp cords, television wires, shoes or table legs. Chewing into a television wire, for example, can be fatal to the puppy, while a shorted wire can start a fire in the house.

If your pup chews on the arm of the chair when he is alone, you probably will discipline him angrily when you get home. Thus, he makes the association that your coming home means he is going to be punished. (He will not remember chewing the chair and is

Having housetraining problems with your husky? Ask other Siberian Husky owners for advice and tips, or post your own success story to give other owners encouragement. Log onto **DogChannel.com/Club-Husky** and click on "Community."

SMART TIP!

When proximity prevents you from going home at lunch or during periods when overtime crops up, make alternative arrangements for getting your puppy out. Hire a pet-sitting or walking service, or enlist the aid of an obliging neighbor.

incapable of making the association of the discipline with his naughty deed.) Maintain control by defining your puppy's area to keep him out of mischief.

SCHEDULE A SOLUTION

A puppy should be taken to his relief area each time he is released from his designated area, after meals, after play sessions and when he first awakens in the morning (at 8 weeks of age, this can mean 5 a.m.!). The puppy will indicate that he's ready "to go" by circling or sniffing busily; do not misinterpret these signs. For a puppy less than 10 weeks of age, a routine of taking him out every hour is necessary. As your puppy grows, he will be able to wait for longer periods of time.

Keep potty trips to your puppy's relief area short. Stay no more than 5 or 6 minutes, and then return to inside the house. If your puppy potties during that time outside, lavishly praise him and then immediately take him indoors. If he does not potty, but he has an accident later when you go back indoors, pick him up, say "No!" and return to his relief area. Wait a few minutes, then return to the house again. Never

hit your Siberian Husky puppy or rub his face in urine or excrement when he has had an accident.

Once indoors, put your puppy in his crate until you have had time to clean up his accident. Then release him to the family area and watch him more closely than before. Chances are, his accident was a result of your not picking up his potty signals or waiting too long before offering him the opportunity to relieve himself. Never hold a grudge against your puppy for accidents.

Let your puppy learn that going outdoors means it is time to relieve himself, not to play. Once trained, he will be able to play indoors and outdoors and still differentiate between the times for play versus the times for relief.

Help your puppy develop regular hours for naps, being alone, playing by himself and just resting — all in his crate. Encourage him to entertain himself while you are busy elsewhere. Let him learn that having you nearby is comforting, but it is not your main purpose in life to provide him with undivided attention.

Each time you put your Siberian Husky puppy in his own area, use the same command, whatever suits you best. Soon he will run to his crate or special area when he hears you say those words.

Remember that one of the primary ingredients in housetraining your puppy is control. Regardless of your lifestyle, there will always be occasions when you will need to have a place where your dog can stay and be happy and safe. Cratetraining is the answer for now and in the future.

A few key elements are really all you need for successful housetraining: consistency, frequency, praise, control and supervision. By following these procedures with a normal, healthy puppy, you and your Siberian Husky will soon be past the stage of accidents and ready to move on to a full and rewarding life together.

Make sure your dog does his business before he romps in the snow. Play can be a reward for pottying, but only after the business is concluded!

10 HOUSETRAINING HOW-TOs

1. Decide where you want your husky to eliminate. Take her there every time until she gets the idea. Pick a spot that's easy to access. Remember, puppies have very little time between "gotta go" and "oops."

2. Teach an elimination cue, such as "go potty" or "get busy." Say this every time you take your Siberian Husky to eliminate. Don't keep chanting the cue, just say it once or twice then keep quiet so you won't distract your dog.

3. Praise calmly when your dog eliminates, but stand there a little longer in case there's more.

4. Keep potty outings for potty only. Take your dog to the designated spot, tell her "go potty" and just stand there. If she needs to eliminate, she will do so within five minutes.

5. Don't punish for potty accidents; punishment can hinder progress. If you catch your husky in the act indoors, verbally interrupt but don't scold. Gently carry or lead your pup to the approved spot, let her finish, then praise.

6. If it's too late to interrupt an accident, scoop the poop or blot up the urine afterward with a paper towel. Immediately take your dog and her deposit (gently!) to the potty area. Place the poop or trace of urine on the ground and praise the pup. If she sniffs at her waste, praise more. Let your husky know you're pleased when her waste is in the proper area.

7. Keep track of when and where your husky eliminates — that will help you anticipate potty times. Regular meals mean regular elimination, so feed your dog scheduled, measured meals instead of free-feeding (leaving food available at all times).

8. Hang a bell on a sturdy cord from the doorknob. Before you open the door to take your puppy out for potty, shake the cord and ring the bell. Most dogs soon realize the connection between the bell ringing and the door opening, then they'll try it out for themselves.

9. Dogs naturally return to re-soil where they've previously eliminated, so thoroughly clean up all accidents. Household cleaners usually will do the job, but special enzyme solutions may work better.

10. If the ground is littered with too much waste, your husky may seek a cleaner place to eliminate. Scoop the potty area daily, leaving behind just one "reminder."

CHAPTER 6

VET VISITS AND

EVERYDAY CARE

Your selection of a veterinarian for your dog should be based on personal recommendations of the doctor's skills, and, if possible, his experience with Siberian Huskies. If the veterinarian is based nearby, it will be helpful and more convenient because you might have an emergency or need to make multiple visits for treatments.

FIRST STEP: SELECT THE RIGHT VET

All licensed veterinarians are capable of dealing with routine medical issues such as infections and injuries, as well as the promotion of good health (like vaccinations). If the problem affecting your husky is more complex, your vet may refer you to someone with more detailed knowledge of what is wrong. This usually will be a specialist such as a veterinary dermatologist or veterinary ophthalmologist.

Veterinary procedures are very costly and, as treatments improve, they are going to become more expensive. It is quite acceptable to discuss matters of cost with your vet; if there is more than one treatment option, cost may be a factor in deciding which route to take.

Smart owners will look for a vet before they actually need one. For new pet owners, start looking for a veterinarian a month or two before you bring home your new Siberian Husky puppy. That will give you time to meet candidate veterinarians, check out the condition of the clinic, meet the staff and see who you feel most comfortable with. If you already have a husky puppy, look sooner rather than later, preferably not in the midst of a veterinary health crisis.

Second, list the qualities that are important to you. Points to consider or investigate:

Convenience: Proximity to your home, extended hours or drop-off services are helpful for people who work regular business hours, have a busy schedule or don't want to drive far. If you have mobility issues, finding a vet who makes house calls or a service that provides pet transport might be particularly important.

Size: A one-person practice will ensure that you will always be dealing with the same vet during each and every visit. "That person can really get to know you and your dog," says Bernadine Cruz, D.V.M., of Laguna Hills Animal Hospital in Laguna Hills, Calif. The downside is that the sole practitioner does not have the immediate input of another vet, and if your vet becomes ill or takes time off, you are out of luck.

A multiple-vet practice offers consistency if your dog needs to unexpectedly come in on a day when your veterinarian isn't there. Additionally, your vet can quickly consult with colleagues within the clinic if unsure about a diagnosis or a treatment.

If you find a veterinarian within that practice who you really like, you can make your appointments with that individual, establishing the same kind of bond that you would with the solo practitioner.

Appointment Policies: Some vet practices are by-appointment only, which could minimize your wait time. However, if a sudden problem arises with your Siberian Husky and the veterinarians are booked up, they might not be able to squeeze your pet in that day. Some clinics are walk-in only, which is great for impromptu or crisis visits, but without scheduling, it may involve longer waits to see the next available veterinarian. Some practices offer the best of both worlds by maintaining an appointment schedule but also by keeping slots open throughout the day for walk-ins.

Basic vs. Full Service vs. State-of-the-Art: A veterinarian practice with high-tech equipment offers greater diagnostic capabilities and treatment options, important for tricky or difficult cases. However, the cost of pricey equipment is passed along to the client, so you could pay more for routine procedures — the bulk of most pets' appoint-

---

ments. Some practices offer boarding, grooming, training classes and other services on the premises — conveniences some pet owners appreciate.

Fees and Payment Polices: How much is a routine visit? If there is a significant price difference, ask why. If you intend to carry health insurance on your Siberian Husky or want to pay by credit card, check that the clinic accepts those payment options.

FIRST VET VISIT

It is much easier, less costly and more effective to practice preventive medicine than to fight bouts of illness and disease. Properly bred puppies of all breeds come from parents who were selected based upon their genetic disease profile. The puppies' mother should have been vaccinated,

free of all internal and external parasites, and properly nourished. For these reasons, a visit to the veterinarian who cared for the mother is recommended if at all possible. The mother passes disease resistance to her puppies, which should last from 8 to 10 weeks. Unfortunately, she can also pass on parasites and infection. This is why knowing about her health is useful in learning more about the health of her puppies.

Once you have your Siberian Husky puppy home safe and sound, it's time to arrange for his first trip to the veterinarian. Perhaps the breeder can recommend someone in the area who specializes in Siberian Huskies, or maybe you know other Siberian Husky owners who can suggest a good vet. Either way, you should make an appointment within a couple of

Regularly scheduled vet visits can help prevent minor problems from becoming larger issues.

days of bringing home your puppy. If possible, see if you can stop for this first vet appointment before going home.

Your puppy's first vet visit will consist of an overall examination to make sure that he does not have any problems that are not apparent to you. The veterinarian also will set up a schedule for your pup's vaccinations; the breeder should inform you of which ones your puppy has already received, and the vet can continue from there.

Your puppy will also have his teeth examined and have his skeletal conformation and general health checked prior to certification by the veterinarian. Puppies in certain breeds have problems with their kneecaps, cataracts and other eye problems, heart murmurs and undescended testicles. They may also have behavioral problems, which your vet can evaluate if he or she has had relevant training.

VACCINATION SCHEDULING

Most vaccinations are given by injection and should only be given by a veterinarian. Both you and the vet should keep a record of the date of the injection, the identification of the vaccine and the amount given. Some vets give a first vaccination at 8 weeks of age, but most breeders prefer the course not to commence until about 10 weeks because of interaction with the antibodies produced by the mother. The vaccination scheduling is usually based on a 15-day cycle. You must take your vet's advice as to when to vaccinate, as this may differ according to the vaccine used.

The usual vaccines contain immunizing doses of several different viruses such as distemper, parvovirus, parainfluenza and hepatitis. There are other vaccines available when the puppy is at a greater risk for viral exposures. You should rely on your vet's advice. This is especially true for the booster immunizations. Most vaccination programs require a booster when the puppy is a year old and once a year thereafter. In some cases, circumstances may require more frequent immunizations.

Set up a vet visit before you even bring your new dog home, so you can interview the veterinary staff.

**Just like with infants, puppies need a series of vaccinations
to ensure that they stay healthy during their first year of life.**
Download a vaccination chart from **DogChannel.com/Club-Husky**
that you can fill out for your Siberian Husky.

Kennel cough, more formally known as *tracheobronchitis*, is combatted with a vaccine that is sprayed into the dog's nostrils. Kennel cough is usually included in routine vaccinations, but it is often not as effective as the vaccines for other major diseases.

Your veterinarian probably will recommend that your Siberian Husky puppy be fully vaccinated before you take him on outings. Airborne diseases, parasite eggs in the grass and unexpected visits from other dogs might be dangerous to your puppy's health. Other dogs are the most harmful reservoir of pathogenic organisms, as everything they have can be transmitted to your puppy.

6 Months to 1 Year of Age: Unless you intend to breed or show your dog, neutering or spaying your Siberian Husky at 6 months of age is recommended. Discuss this with your veterinarian. Neutering and spaying have proven to be beneficial to male and female puppies, respectively. Besides eliminating the possibility of pregnancy, it inhibits (but does not prevent) breast cancer in females and prostate cancer in male dogs.

Your veterinarian should provide your Siberian Husky puppy with a thorough dental evaluation at 6 months of age, ascertaining whether all his permanent teeth have erupted properly. A home dental care regimen should be initiated at 6 months, including weekly brushing and providing good dental devices (such as nylon bones). Regular dental care promotes healthy teeth, fresh breath and a longer life.

Dogs Older Than 1 Year: Continue to visit the veterinarian at least once a year as bodily functions do change with age. The eyes and ears are no longer as efficient; liver, kidney and intestinal functions often decline. Proper dietary changes recommended by your veterinarian can make life more pleasant for your aging Siberian Husky and you.

EVERYDAY HAPPENINGS

Keeping your Siberian Husky healthy is a matter of keen observation and quick action when necessary. Knowing what's normal for your dog will help you recognize signs of trouble before they blos-

Smart owners won't pick just any vet out of the phone book; they will invest time in researching and interviewing the best vet for their dog.

The Siberian Husky Ophthalmologic Registry was established by the Siberian Husky Club of America in 1979. A registry for Siberians older than 1 year of age that have been examined and found free of eye defects by an American College of Veterinary Ophthalmology diplomate, SHOR was founded when Canine Eye Registration Foundation disbanded for a brief period.

When selecting a vet for your dog, make sure he or she is familiar with Siberian Huskies.

Siberians R Super

Hooray 4 Huskies!

som into a full-blown emergency situation. Even if the problem is minor, such as a cut or scrape, you'll want to care for it immediately to prevent infection, as well as to ensure that your Siberian Husky doesn't make it worse by chewing or scratching at it. Here's what to do for common, minor injuries or illnesses, and how to recognize and deal with emergencies.

Cuts and Scrapes: For a cut or scrape that's half an inch or smaller, clean the wound with saline solution or warm water and use tweezers to remove any splinters or other debris. Apply an antibiotic ointment. No bandage is necessary unless the wound is on a paw, which can pick up dirt when your dog walks on it. Deep cuts with lots of bleeding or those caused by glass or some other object should be treated by your veterinarian.

Cold Symptoms: Dogs don't actually get colds, but they can get illnesses that have similar symptoms, such as coughing, a runny nose or sneezing. Dogs cough for any number of reasons, from respiratory infections to inhaled irritants to congestive heart failure. Take your Siberian Husky to the veterinarian for prolonged coughing, or coughing accompanied by labored breathing, runny eyes and nose or bloody phlegm.

Stay on top of your dog's health by keeping a record of his vaccinations.

it's a Fact **All Siberian Huskies need exercise to keep them physically and mentally healthy.** An inactive dog is an overweight dog, who will likely suffer joint strain or torn ligaments. Inactive dogs also are prone to mischief and may do anything to relieve their boredom. This often leads to behavioral problems, such as chewing or barking. Regular daily exercise, such as walks and play sessions, will keep your Siberian Husky slim, trim and happy.

A runny nose that continues for more than several hours requires veterinary attention, as well. If your Siberian Husky sneezes, he may have some mild nasal irritation that will resolve on its own, but frequent sneezing, especially if it's accompanied by a runny nose, may indicate anything from allergies to an infection or something stuck in his nose.

Vomiting and Diarrhea: Sometimes dogs can suffer minor gastric upset when they eat a new type of food, eat too much, eat the contents of the trash can or become excited or anxious. Give your Siberian Husky's stomach a rest by withholding food for 12 hours, and then feeding him a bland diet such as baby food or rice and chicken, gradually returning your dog to his normal food. Projectile vomiting or vomiting or diarrhea that continues for more than 48 hours, is another matter. If this happens, immediately take your Siberian Husky to the veterinarian.

MORE HEALTH HINTS

A Siberian Husky's anal glands can cause problems if not periodically evacuated. In the wild, dogs regularly clear their anal glands to mark their territory. In domestic dogs this function is no longer necessary; thus, their contents can build up and clog, causing discomfort. Signs that the anal glands — located on both sides of the anus — need emptying are if your dog drags his rear end along the ground or keeps turning around to lick the area of discomfort.

While care must be taken not to cause injury, anal glands can be evacuated by pressing gently on either side of the anal opening and by using a piece of cotton or a tissue to collect the foul-smelling matter. If anal glands are allowed to become impacted, abscesses can form, causing pain and the need for veterinary attention.

Siberian Huskies can get into all sorts of mischief, so it is not uncommon for them to swallow something poisonous in the course of their investigations. Obviously, an urgent visit to the vet is required under such circumstances, but if possible, when you call your vet, inform him which poisonous substance has been ingested, because different treatments may be needed. Should it be necessary to cause your dog to vomit (which is not always the case with poisoning), a small lump of baking soda, given orally, will have an immediate effect. A small teaspoon of salt or mustard, dissolved in water, will have a similar effect but may be more difficult to administer and take longer to work.

Siberian Husky puppies often have painful fits while they are teething. These are not usually serious and are brief. Of course, you must be certain that the cause is nothing more than teething. Giving a puppy something hard to chew on will usually solve this temporary problem.

Did You Know?

Obesity is linked to the earlier onset of age-related health problems. Keep your dog's weight in line by providing sufficient exercise and play and by feeding proper serving sizes. Because calorie requirements decline as your puppy reaches adulthood, and can drop 25 to 30 percent within a couple of months after spaying/neutering, you'll probably need to reduce serving portions and switch to a less calorie-dense diet.

No matter how careful you are with your precious Siberian Husky, sometimes unexpected injuries happen. Be prepared for an emergency by creating a canine first-aid kit. Find out what essentials you need on **DogChannel.com/Club-Husky** — just click on "Downloads."

JOIN OUR ONLINE
Club Husky™

Bred for strength and stamina, the Siberian is a hardy breed. However, no breed of dog — indeed, no animal, including humans — is completely free of the genetic defects that can cause hereditary disease. Hip dysplasia, cataracts and progressive retinal atrophy are among the genetic diseases that most concern Siberian fanciers. Fortunately, these diseases are not a major problem in Siberian Huskies, but every owner should be aware of them, as well as other health issues, such as parasites and allergies.

CHRONIC HIP DYSPLASIA

Chronic hip dysplasia is the No. 1 genetic health problem in dogs, and the Siberian Husky is no exception. Chronic hip dysplasia results in a loose hip joint and abnormal rubbing of the joint surfaces. The joint eventually becomes inflamed, causing chronic pain and even the development of arthritis.

Clinical signs of hip dysplasia include limping, difficulty getting up, stiffness, altered gait, struggling to go up stairs or get into the car, and reduced interest in play. Treatment options vary depending upon the type of symptoms your dog experiences, his age and when he is diagnosed. Conservative treatments for mildly dysplastic dogs include:

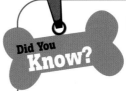

Did You Know?

Dogs can get many diseases from ticks, including Lyme disease, Rocky Mountain spotted fever, tick bite paralysis and many others.

● weight control. Shedding extra pounds is often enough to decrease or eliminate joint pain in dogs.

● prescription diets to help improve joint function. Choose a formula that contains omega-3 fatty acids for best results. Some of these formulas also contain glucosamine and chondroitin, although the amounts may not be adequate, according to Darryl Millis, D.V.M., who is also a professor of orthopedic surgery at the University of Tennessee, Knoxville. "These diets replace the need for separate supplementation with omega-3 fatty acids," Millis says.

● glucosamine/chondroitin supplements to promote joint health (if not provided in adequate amounts in your Siberian Husky's diet). Studies in arthritic humans found that glucosamine/chondroitin supplements helped those with moderate to severe knee pain However, well-controlled, long-term studies are still needed in clinically affected animals.

● pain-relief drugs (anti-inflammatories prescribed under veterinary supervision). Some dogs show better results with one medication over another, so you may have to try a couple of different types before finding one that works best for your dog.

● regular exercise to maintain muscle tone, strength and range of motion in the joint. Regular, low-impact activity such as swimming or leash walks at a speed and distance your dog can handle (not to the point of lameness or stiffness) are recommended. Another good exercise is "dancing" the dog frontward. "Pick up the dog's forelimbs and walk him forward as you walk backward," Millis explains. "This strengthens the gluteal muscles and helps reduce arthritis pain. But don't walk the dog backward, as this could cause hip pain

A Siberian's eyes are amazing to look at, but they can have health issues, including cataracts.

because of the more extended position of the hip joint."

● TENS (transcutaneous electrical nerve stimulation), a device that uses electrical impulse to reduce pain. "We found positive response to that," Millis says. "Most treatments last 20 to 30 minutes."

● ESWT (extracorporeal shockwave therapy), a treatment that uses sound waves to induce pain relief. "We tested dogs who were pretty bad and found, in general, a single treatment lasted several months," Millis says. Studies elsewhere found that less severely affected dogs achieved pain relief for up to two years.

More severely affected dogs as well as young dogs may best be served by surgical procedures. Surgical options include:

▲ Juvenile Pubic Symphysidesis. If diagnosed before a puppy reaches 14 to 16 weeks of age, this simple, minimally invasive procedure can be performed, often in combination with an early spay or neuter. With this procedure, growing cartilage cells in the lower pelvis are cauterized to create a tighter hip joint. "Most puppies aren't symptomatic by that age," Millis notes, "but for high-risk dogs or loose-hipped puppies, it may be beneficial to perform JPS prophylactically during a spay or neuter."

▲ Triple Pelvic Osteotomy. The pelvic bone is cut in three places and repositioned to better secure the hip femoral head. "TPO is best performed in growing dogs with minimal or no arthritic changes," Millis states. "It doesn't work as well after arthritic changes have occurred. That's a mistake some dog owners make: They adopt a wait-and-see attitude and in as little as two to four weeks, they lose their window of opportunity for that procedure."

▲ femoral head and neck incision. Best for dogs weighing less than 50 pounds, this

An active breed like the Siberian isn't immune to genetic problems, such as hip dysplasia.

technique removes the femoral head and neck, forming a false joint.

▲ hip replacement surgery. Although expensive, hip replacement surgery provides your dog with a functional, albeit artificial, hip. "Many dogs with a hip replacement have a profound improvement in their quality of their life," Millis reports.

Prognosis varies, depending upon treatment options and the severity of the disease. Mildly affected dogs can often be successfully managed with conservative treatments for a long time. The outlook for hip repair and reconstruction generally ranges from good to excellent.

Although hip dysplasia is a genetic disorder, other causes include overfeeding and over- or under-supplementation of carbohydrates, calcium and phosphorous in growing dogs. Talk with your veterinarian to find the appropriate diet formula for your puppy or adolescent dog.

EYE PROBLEMS

Few could argue that the eyes of the Siberian Husky are one of the breed's most attractive features. It is indeed ironic that the breeders should be concerned about preserving the vision of the exquisite eyes of the husky. Nonetheless, eye problems are the most prevalent of all disorders in the breed. Potential owners are not to be discouraged by this information. The incidence of problems is indeed low for the breed in general, maybe five percent, but a smart owner should still be aware of the following eye issues.

◆ **Glaucoma** is a buildup of pressure in the dog's eyeball. The eyeball's drainage channel becomes narrow, and eventually blocked, and the increase in pressure can result in blindness. All Siberian Huskies should be tested for glaucoma at one year of age, and if it is indicated that he is predisposed for glaucoma, then he cannot be bred. Dogs that are labeled "predisposed" must be tested annually, and dogs that actually develop glaucoma are labeled "affected."

◆ **Hereditary cataracts** cause a cloudiness in the eye that can lead to blindness. This can be operated on, but the dog's sight cannot be restored to that of a normal dog. Annual checkups will help detect cataracts, and an affected dog should not be bred. Bilateral cataracts, also known as juvenile cataracts, occur in younger dogs, and are hereditary in the Siberian Husky. In huskies, the most commonly identified cataracts are found in the posterior axial subcapsular region of the lens. Such cataracts mature as the dog grows. In certain cases, the cataract can be detected in one eye before the other eye appears affected. In severe cases, the dog can go blind because of the intensity of the opacities in the eyes.

◆ **Corneal dystrophy** is a condition that has similar symptoms to those of cataracts in that the dog's eye gets cloudy and his vision becomes blocked. The preferred veterinary term for the condition is crystalline corneal opacities. This term describes the cone-shaped crystals that are produced in the cornea and that spread across the surface, potentially interfering with the dog's vision. Both eyes are affected by CCO, as in bilateral cataracts, though not simultaneously or to the same degree in every incidence.

◆ **Progressive retinal atrophy** is an inherited problem that eventually causes total blindness and is a family of possibly up to 30 related eye diseases. "PRA initially affects a dog's ability to see in the dark," says

Gustavo D. Aguirre, V.M.D., Ph.D., professor of ophthalmology and director of the Center for Canine Genetics and Reproduction at Cornell University's James A. Baker Institute for Animal Health. "Later, the dog loses daytime vision, then he becomes blind. The age at which a dog develops blindness is very specific to the breed and the type of disease." There is no treatment, but according to the Siberian Husky Club of America, incidence in the breed is low.

In most breeds, PRA is passed along via simple autosomal recessive genes: The offspring must inherit a defective version of the gene from both parents to be affected, but it may be a carrier if only one defective gene is inherited. However, in the Siberian Husky, the disease is inherited differently. "There is one form of

PRA, XLPRA in Siberian Huskies, that does not follow the pattern of autosomal-recessive inheritance. XLPRA is an X-linked, rather than an autosomally inherited, disease," Aguirre explains.

"Since the X and Y sex chromosomes are distributed unequally to males (XY) and females (XX), X-linked diseases appear with unequal frequency in the two sexes. Males are either genetically normal or they are affected. Three possible states — normal, carrier and affected — exist for females."

This means that males who inherit a defective X chromosome from their mothers will be affected by the disease. Females must inherit defective X chromosomes from both parents in order to be affected. "Although it might seem illogical at first," Aguirre adds, "the male progeny of an affected sire are at no increased risk of inheriting XLPRA because only the female offspring will inherit his defective X chromosome. The males inherit his normal Y."

Because the age of onset or clinical signs of PRA may not occur until after a dog has produced many litters, a breeder could unknowingly perpetuate the disease in that line. Certainly knowing the family history of a dog helps, although family history alone cannot always identify carriers or affected dogs that have an absence of clinical signs.

OTHER HEALTH CONCERNS

Airborne allergies: Just as humans suffer from hay fever during allergy season, many dogs suffer from the same. When the pollen count is high, your husky might suffer, but don't expect him to sneeze or have a runny nose like a human. Huskies react to airborne allergies in the same way they react to parasite bites; they scratch and bite themselves. Dogs, like humans, can be tested for allergies. Be sure to discuss allergy testing with your vet.

Autoimmune illness: An autoimmune illness is one in which the immune system overacts and does not recognize parts of the affected person. Instead, the immune system starts to react as if these parts were foreign cells and need to be destroyed. An example of an autoimmune illness is rheumatoid arthritis, which occurs when the body does not recognize the joints. This leads to a very painful and damaging reaction in the joints. Rheumatoid arthritis has nothing to do with age, so it can also occur in puppies. The wear-and-tear arthritis in older people or dogs is called osteoarthritis.

Lupus is another autoimmune disease that affects dogs as well as people. It can take variable forms, affecting the kidneys, bones and skin. It can be fatal, so it is treated with steroids, which have very significant side effects. Steroids calm down the allergic reaction to the body's tissues, which helps the lupus, but also affects the body's reaction to actual foreign cells such as bacteria; they also thins the skin and bones.

Food allergies: Properly feeding your husky is very important. An incorrect diet could affect your dog's health, behavior and nervous system, possibly making a normal dog aggressive. The result of a good or bad diet is most visible in a dog's skin and coat, but the internal organs are affected, too.

Dogs are allergic to many foods that are popular and highly recommended by breeders and veterinarians. Changing the brand of food may not eliminate the problem if the ingredient to which your dog is allergic is contained in the new brand.

Recognizing a food allergy can be difficult. Humans often have rashes or swelling of the lips or eyes when they eat foods they are allergic to. Dogs do not usually develop rashes, but they react the same way they do to an airborne allergy or parasite bite; they itch, scratch and bite. While pollen allergies and parasite bites are usually seasonal, food allergies are year-round problems.

Diagnosis of a food allergy is based on a two- to four-week dietary trial with a home-cooked diet, excluding all other foods. The diet should consist of boiled rice or potato with a source of protein that your husky has never eaten before, such as fresh or frozen fish, lamb or even something as exotic as pheasant. Water has to be the only drink, and it is important that no other foods are fed during this trial. If your dog's condition improves, try the original diet again to see if the itching resumes. If it does, then your dog is allergic to his original diet. You must find a diet that does not distress your dog's skin. Start with a commercially available hypoallergenic food or the homemade diet that you created for the allergy trial.

Food intolerance is the dog's inability to completely digest certain foods. This occurs because the dog does not have the enzymes necessary to digest some foodstuffs. All puppies have the enzymes needed to digest canine milk, but some dogs do not have the enzymes to digest cow milk, resulting in loose bowels, stomach pains and flatulence.

Dogs often do not have the enzymes to digest soy or other beans. The treatment is to exclude these foods from your husky's diet.

EXTERNAL PARASITES

Insect bites itch, erupt and can become infected. Dogs have the same reaction to fleas, ticks and mites. When an insect lands on you, you can whisk it away. Unfortunately, when your husky is bitten by a flea, tick or mite, he can only scratch or bite.

By the time your husky has been bitten, the parasite has done its damage. It may have laid eggs, which will cause further problems. The itching from parasite bites is probably due to the saliva injected into the site when the parasite sucks the dog's blood.

Fleas: Of all the health and grooming problems to which canines are susceptible, none is better known and more frustrating than fleas. Flea infestation is relatively simple to cure but difficult to prevent.

To control flea infestation, you have to understand the flea's life cycle. Fleas are often thought of as a summertime problem, but centrally heated homes have made fleas a year-round issue. The most effective method of flea control is a two-stage approach: kill the adult fleas, then control the development of *pupae* (pre-adult) fleas. Unfortunately, no single active ingredient is effective against all stages of the flea life cycle.

Treating fleas should be a two-pronged attack. First, the environment needs to be treated; this includes carpets and furniture, especially your Mini's bedding and areas underneath furniture. The environment should be treated with a household spray containing an insect growth regulator and an insecticide to kill the adult fleas. Most insecticides are effective against eggs and larvae; they actually mimic the fleas' own hormones and stop the eggs and larvae from developing into adult fleas. There are currently no treatments available to attack the *pupae* stage of the life cycle, so the adult insecticide is used to kill the newly hatched adult fleas before they find a host. Most insect growth regulators are active for many months, while adult insecticides are only active for a few days.

When treating fleas with a household spray, vacuum before applying the product. This stimulates as many *pupae* as possible to hatch into adult fleas. The vacuum cleaner should also be treated with an insecticide to prevent the eggs and larvae that have been collected in the vacuum bag from hatching.

The second stage of treatment is to apply an adult insecticide to your Siberian Husky. Traditionally, this would be in the form of a collar or a spray. Recent innovations include digestible insecticides that poison the fleas when they ingest the dog's blood. Alternatively, there are drops that, when placed on the back of the dog's neck,

Fleas aren't fun for anyone, but they can and do occur, to the dismay of everyone.

spread throughout the hair and skin to kill adult fleas.

Ticks: Though not as common as fleas, ticks are found all over the tropical and temperate world. They don't bite like fleas; they harpoon. They dig their sharp *proboscis* (nose) into the husky's skin and drink the blood, which is their only food and drink. Ticks are controlled the same way fleas are controlled.

The American dog tick, *Dermacentor variabilis*, may be the most common dog tick in many areas, especially those areas where the climate is hot and humid. Most dog ticks have life expectancies of a week to 6 months, depending on climatic conditions. They can neither jump nor fly, but they can crawl slowly and can travel up to 16 feet to reach a sleeping or unsuspecting dog.

Mites: Just as fleas and ticks can be problematic for your dog, mites can also lead to an itch fit. Microscopic in size, mites are related to ticks and generally take up permanent residence on their host animal — in this case, a husky. The term "mange" refers to any infestation caused by one of the mighty mites, of which there are six varieties that smart dog owners should know about.

■ Demodex mites cause a condition known as *demodicosis* (sometimes called "red mange" or "follicular mange"), in which the mites live in the dog's hair follicles and sebaceous glands in larger-than-normal numbers. Most dogs recover from this type of mange without any treatment, though topical therapies are commonly prescribed by a veterinarian.

■ The *Cheyletiellosis* mite is the hook-mouthed culprit associated with "walking dandruff," a condition that affects dogs as well as cats and rabbits. If untreated, this mange can affect a whole kennel of dogs and can be spread to humans as well.

■ The *Sarcoptes* mite causes intense itching on the dog in the form of a condition known as scabies or sarcoptic mange. Scabies is highly contagious and can be passed to humans. Sometimes an allergic reaction to the mite worsens the severe itching associated with sarcoptic mange.

■ Ear mites, *Otodectes cynotis*, lead to otodectic mange, which commonly affects the outer ear canal of the dog, though other areas can be affected as well. Your vet can prescribe a treatment to flush out the ears and kill any eggs. A complete month of treatment is necessary to cure this mange.

■ Two other mites, less common in dogs, include *Dermanyssus gallinae* (the "poultry" or "red" mite) and *Eutrombicula alfreddugesi* (the North American mite associated with *trombiculidiasis* or chigger infestation). The types of mange caused by both of these mites must be treated by vets.

INTERNAL PARASITES

Most animals — fish, birds and mammals, including dogs and humans — have worms and other parasites that live inside their bodies. According to Dr. Herbert R. Axelrod, a fish pathologist, there are two kinds of parasites: "smart" and "dumb." The smart parasites live in peaceful cooperation with

After an outing with your dog, be sure to check for any ticks that might have hitched a ride.

Brush your dog's teeth every day. Plaque colonizes on the tooth surface in as little as six to eight hours, and if not removed by brushing, forms calculus (tartar) within three to five days. Plaque and tartar cause gum disease, periodontal disease, loosening of the teeth and tooth loss. In bad cases of dental disease, bacteria from the mouth can get into the bloodstream, leading to kidney or heart problems — all of which are life-shortening problems.

their hosts — a symbiotic relationship — while the dumb parasites kill their hosts. Most worm infections are relatively easy to control. If they are not controlled, they weaken the host dog to the point that other medical problems occur, but they do not kill the host as dumb parasites would.

Roundworms: They live in the dog's intestines and continually shed eggs. It has been estimated that a dog produces more than six ounces of feces every day; each ounce averages hundreds of thousands of roundworm eggs when the dog is infected. There are no known areas in which dogs roam that do not contain roundworm eggs. Roundworms infect people, too, so have your dog regularly tested.

A roundworm infection can kill puppies and cause severe problems in adult dogs, as the hatched larvae travel to the lungs and trachea through the bloodstream. Cleanliness is the best prevention against roundworms. Always pick up after your dog and dispose of feces in appropriate receptacles.

Hookworms: Hookworms are dangerous to humans as well as to dogs and cats, and can be the cause of severe iron-deficiency anemia. The worm uses its teeth to attach itself to the dog's intestines and changes the site of its attachment about six times per day. Each time the worm repositions itself, the dog loses blood and can become anemic.

Symptoms of hookworm infection include dark stools, weight loss, general weakness, pale coloration and anemia, as well as possible skin problems. Fortunately, hookworms are easily purged with a number of medications that have proven effective. Discuss these with your veterinarian. Most heartworm preventive medicines include a hookworm insecticide.

Humans, can be infected by hookworms through exposure to contaminated feces. Because the worms cannot complete their life cycle in a human, the worms simply infest the skin and cause irritation. As a preventive, use disposable gloves or a poop scoop to pick up your husky's droppings and prevent your dog (or neighborhood cats) from defecating in children's play areas.

Tapeworms: There are many species of tapeworms, all of which are carried by fleas. Fleas are so small that your husky could pass them onto your hands, your plate or your food, making it possible for you to ingest a flea that is carrying tapeworm eggs. While a tapeworm infection is not life-threatening in dogs (it's a *smart* parasite), if transmitted to humans, it can be the cause of a serious liver disease.

Whipworms: In North America, whipworms are counted among the most common parasitic worms in dogs. Affected dogs may only experience upset tummies, colic and diarrhea. These worms, however, can live for months or years in the dog, beginning their larval stage in the small intestine, spending their adult life in the large intestine and finally passing infective eggs through the dog's feces. The only way to detect whipworms is through a fecal examination, though this is not always foolproof. Treatment for whipworms is tricky, due to the worms' unusual life cycle, and often dogs are reinfected due to exposure to infective eggs on the ground. Cleaning up droppings in your backyard and in public places is necessary for sanitary purposes and the health of your dog and others.

Threadworms: Though less common than roundworms and hookworms, threadworms concern dog owners in the southwestern United States and the Gulf Coast area where the climate is hot and humid, which is the prime environment for threadworms. Living in the small intestine of the dog, this worm measures a mere two millimeters and is round in shape. Like the whipworm, the threadworm's life cycle is very complex and the eggs and larvae are transported through the feces.

A deadly disease in humans, threadworms readily infect people, mostly through the handling of feces. Threadworms are most often seen in young puppies. The most common symptoms include bloody diarrhea and pneumonia. Infected puppies must be promptly isolated and treated to prevent spreading the threadworms to other dogs and humans; vets recommend a follow-up treatment one month later.

Heartworms: These thin, extended worms that measure up to 12 inches long and live in a dog's heart and inhabit the major blood vessels around it. Dogs may have up to 200 heartworms. Symptoms may be loss of energy, loss of appetite, coughing, the development of a pot belly and anemia.

Heartworms are transmitted by mosquitoes, which drink the blood of infected dogs and take in larvae with the blood. The larvae,

called *microfilariae*, develop within the body of the mosquito and are then passed on to the next dog bitten after the larvae mature.

It takes two to three weeks for the larvae to develop to the infective stage within the body of the mosquito. Dogs are usually treated at about 6 weeks of age and are maintained on a prophylactic dose given monthly to regulate proliferation.

Although this is a dangerous disease, it is difficult for a dog to be infected. Discuss the various preventives with your veterinarian, because there are many different types now available. Together, you can decide on a safe course of prevention for your Siberian Husky.

Y ou have probably heard it a thousand times: You are what you eat. Believe it or not, it is very true. For Siberian Huskies, they are what you feed them because they have little choice in the matter. Even smart owners who want to feed their huskies the best often cannot do so because it can be so confusing. With the overwhelming assortment of dog foods available, it's difficult to figure out which one is truly best for their dogs.

BASIC TYPES

Dog foods are produced in various types: dry, wet, semimoist and frozen.

Dry food is useful for cost-conscious owners because it tends to be less expensive than the others. These foods also contain the least fat and the most preservatives. Dry food is bulky and takes longer to eat than other foods, so it's more filling.

Wet food — available in cans or foil pouches — is usually 60 to 70 percent water and is more expensive than dry food. A palatable source of concentrated nutrition, wet food also makes a good supplement for underweight dogs or those recovering from illnesses. Some smart owners add a little wet food to dry food to increase its appeal.

it's a **Fact** Bones can cause gastro-intestinal obstruction and perforation, and may be contaminated with salmonella or E. coli. Leave them in the trash and give your dog a nylon bone toy instead.

Semimoist food is flavorful, but it usually contains lots of sugar, which can lead to dental problems and obesity. Therefore, semimoist food is not a good choice for your Siberian Husky's main diet.

Likewise, **frozen food**, which is available in cooked and in raw forms, is usually more expensive than wet foods. The advantages of frozen food are similar to those of wet foods.

The amount of food that your Siberian Husky needs depends on a number of factors, such as his age, activity level, the quality of the food, reproductive status (if your husky is a female) and size. What's the easiest way to figure it out? Start with the manufacturer's recommended amount, then adjust it according to your dog's response. For example, feed the recommended amount for a few weeks, and if your Siberian loses weight, increase the amount by 10 to 20 percent. If your Siberian Husky gains weight, decrease the amount. It won't take long to determine the amount of food that keeps your best friend in optimal condition.

NUTRITION 101

All huskies (and all dogs, for that matter) need proteins, carbohydrates, fats, vitamins and minerals to be in peak condition.

■ **Proteins** are used for growth and repair of muscles, bones and other tissues. They're also used for the production of antibodies, enzymes and hormones. All dogs need protein, but it's especially important for puppies because they grow and develop so quickly. Protein sources include various types of meat, meat meal, meat byproducts, eggs and dairy products.

■ **Carbohydrates** are metabolized into glucose, the body's principal energy source. Carbohydrates are available as sugars, starches and fiber.

• Sugars (simple carbohydrates) are not suitable nutrient sources for dogs.

• Starches — a preferred carbohydrate in dog food — are found in a variety of plant products. Starches must be cooked in order to be digested.

• Fiber (cellulose) — also a preferred type of carbohydrate found in dog food — isn't digestible, but helps the digestive tract function properly.

■ **Fats** are also a source of energy and play an important role in maintaining your husky's skin and coat health, hormone production, nervous system function and vitamin transport. However, you must be aware that fats increase the palatability and the calorie count of dog food, which can lead to serious health problems, such as obesity, for puppies or dogs who are

Believe it or not, during your husky's lifetime, you'll buy a few thousand pounds of dog food! Go to **DogChannel.com/Club-Husky** and download a chart that outlines the cost of dog food.

allowed to overindulge. Some foods contain added amounts of omega fatty acids such as docosohexaenoic acid, a compound that may enhance brain development and learning in puppies but is not considered an essential nutrient by the Association of American Feed Control Officials. Fats used in dog foods include tallow, lard, poultry fat, fish oil and vegetable oils.

■ **Vitamins** and **minerals** are essential to dogs for proper muscle and nerve function, bone growth, healing, metabolism and fluid balance. Especially important for your husky puppy are calcium, phosphorus and vitamin D, which must be supplied in the right balance to ensure proper development and maintenance of bones and teeth.

Just as your dog receives proper nutrition from his food, water is an essential nutrient, as well. Water keeps your dog's body hydrated and facilitates normal function of the body's systems. During housetraining, it is necessary to keep an eye on how much water your Siberian Husky is drinking, but once he is reliably trained, he should have access to clean, fresh water at all times, especially if you feed him dry food. Make sure that your dog's water bowl is clean, and change the water often.

CHECK OUT THE LABEL

To help you get a feel for what you are feeding your dog, start by taking a look at the label on the package or can. Look for the words "complete and balanced." This tells you that the food meets specific nutritional requirements set by the AAFCO for either adults (maintenance) or puppies and pregnant/lactating females (growth and reproduction). The label must state the group for which the food is intended. If you're feeding a puppy, choose a growth and reproduction food.

The nutrition label also includes a list of minimum protein, minimum fat, maximum fiber and maximum moisture content. (You won't find carbohydrate content because it's everything that isn't protein, fat, fiber and moisture.)

The nutritional analysis refers to crude protein and crude fat — amounts that have been determined in the laboratory. This analysis is technically accurate, but it does not tell you anything about digestibility: how

Dogs of all ages love treats and table food, but these goodies can unbalance your Siberian Husky's diet and lead to a weight problem if you don't feed him wisely. Table food, whether fed as a treat or as part of a meal, shouldn't account for more than 10 percent of your dog's daily caloric intake. If you plan to give your Siberian Husky treats, be sure to include "treat calories" when calculating the daily food requirement — so you don't end up with a pudgy pup!

When shopping for packaged treats, look for ones that provide complete nutrition. They're basically dog food in a fun form. Choose crunchy goodies for chewing fun and dental health. Other ideas for tasty treats include:

✓ small chunks of cooked, lean meat
✓ dry dog food morsels
✓ cheese
✓ veggies (cooked, raw or frozen)
✓ breads, crackers or dry cereal
✓ unsalted, unbuttered, plain, popped popcorn

Some foods, however, can be dangerous or even deadly to a dog. The following can cause digestive upset (vomiting or diarrhea) or fatal toxic reactions:

✗ **avocados:** if eaten in sufficient quantity these can cause gastrointestinal irritation, with vomiting and diarrhea

✗ **baby food:** may contain onion powder; does not provide balanced nutrition

✗ **chocolate:** contains methylxanthines and theobromine, caffeine-like compounds that can cause vomiting, diarrhea, heart abnormalities, tremors, seizures and death. Darker chocolates contain higher levels of the toxic compounds.

✗ **eggs, raw:** Whites contain an enzyme that prevents uptake of biotin, a B vitamin; may contain salmonella.

✗ **garlic (and related foods):** can cause gastrointestinal irritation and anemia if eaten in sufficient quantity

✗ **grapes:** can cause kidney failure if eaten in sufficient quantity (the toxic dose varies from dog to dog)

✗ **macadamia nuts:** can cause vomiting, weakness, lack of coordination and other problems

✗ **meat, raw:** may contain harmful bacteria such as salmonella or E. coli

✗ **milk:** can cause diarrhea in some puppies

✗ **onions (and related foods):** can cause gastrointestinal irritation and anemia if eaten in sufficient quantity

✗ **raisins:** can cause kidney failure if eaten in sufficient quantity (the toxic dose varies from dog to dog)

✗ **yeast bread dough:** can rise in the gastrointestinal tract, causing obstruction; produces alcohol as it rises

much of the particular nutrient your Siberian Husky can actually use. For information about digestibility, contact the manufacturer (check the label for a telephone number and website address).

Virtually all commercial puppy foods exceed AAFCO's minimum requirements for protein and fat, the two nutrients most commonly evaluated when comparing foods. Protein levels in dry puppy foods usually range from about 26 to 30 percent; for canned foods, the values are about 9 to 13 percent. The fat content of dry puppy foods is about 20 percent or more; for canned foods, it's 8 percent or more. (Dry food values are larger than canned food values because dry food contains less water; the values are actually similar when compared on a dry matter basis.)

Finally, check the ingredients on the label, which lists the ingredients in descending order by weight. Manufacturers are allowed to list separately different forms of a single ingredient (e.g., ground corn and corn

gluten meal). The food may contain meat byproducts, meat and bone meal, and animal fat, which probably won't appeal to you but are nutritious and safe for your puppy. Higher quality foods usually have meat or meat products near the top of the ingredient list, but you don't need to worry about grain products as long as the label indicates that the food is nutritionally complete. Dogs are omnivores (not carnivores, as commonly believed), so all balanced dog foods contain animal and plant ingredients.

STORE IT RIGHT

Properly storing your Siberian Husky's food will ensure that it maintains its quality, nutrient content and taste. Here's what to do before and after you open that package or can.

◆ Dry food should be stored in a cool, dry, bug- and vermin-free place, especially if it's a preservative-free product. Many manufacturers include an expiration date on the package label, but this usually refers to the shelf life of the unopened package. For optimal quality, don't buy more dry food than your Siberian Husky can eat in one month. To store dry food after opening the bag, fold the bag top down several times and secure it

Your Siberian Husky can't read the labels, so he looks to you to provide the best possible nutrition that you can afford.

Feeding your husky is part of your daily routine. Take a break, and have some fun online and play "Feed the Husky," an exclusive game found only on **DogChannel.com/Club-Husky** — just click on "Games."

How can you tell if your Siberian Husky is fit or fat? When you run your hands down your pal's sides from front to back, you should be able to easily feel her ribs. It's OK if you feel a little body fat (and a lot of hair), but you shouldn't feel huge fat pads. You should also be able to feel your husky's waist — an indentation behind the ribs.

with a clip or empty the contents into a food-grade airtight plastic container (available at pet-supply and discount stores). Make sure the storage container is clean and dry and has never been used to store toxic materials.

◆ Canned food, if unopened, can remain good for three years or longer, but it's best to use it within one year of purchase. Discard puffy cans or those that are leaking fluid. Leftover canned food should be covered and refrigerated, then used within three days.

◆ Frozen food can be stored for at least one year in the freezer. Longer storage can cause deterioration of the quality and taste of the food. Thaw frozen food in the refrigerator or use the defrost setting on your microwave. Cover and refrigerate leftovers, which should be used within 24 hours.

STAGES OF LIFE

When selecting your dog's diet, three stages of development must be considered: the puppy stage, the adult stage and the senior stage.

Puppy Diets: Pups instinctively want to nurse, and a normal puppy will exhibit this behavior from just a few moments following birth. Puppies should be allowed to nurse for about the first six weeks, although by the third or fourth week, the breeder will begin to introduce small portions of a suitable solid food. Most breeders like to initially introduce alternate milk and meat meals, leading up to weaning time.

By the time Siberian Husky puppies are 7 weeks old (or a maximum of 8), they should be fully weaned and fed solely on puppy food. Selection of the most suitable, high-quality food at this time is essential because a puppy's fastest growth rate is during his first year of life. Seek advice about your dog's diet from your veterinarian. The frequency of meals will be reduced over time, and when a young dog has reached 10 to 12 months, he should be switched to an adult diet.

Puppy and junior diets can be well balanced for the needs of your Siberian Husky so that, except in certain circumstances, additional vitamin, mineral and protein supplements will not be required.

How often should you feed your Siberian Husky in a day? Puppies have small stomachs and high metabolic rates, so they need to eat several times a day to consume sufficient nutrients. If your puppy is younger than 3 months old, feed him four or five meals a day. When your Siberian Husky is 3 to 5 months old, decrease the number of meals to three or four. At 6 months, most puppies can move to an adult schedule of two meals a day.

Adult Diets: A dog is considered an adult when he has stopped growing. Rely on your veterinarian or dietary specialist to recommend an acceptable maintenance diet. Major dog food manufacturers specialize in this type of food, and smart owners must select the one best suited to their dogs' needs. Do not leave food out all day for free-choice feeding, as this freedom inevitably translates to inches around your dog's waist.

A healthy dog needs access to plenty of fresh, clean water all day long.

Senior Diets: As dogs get older, their metabolism begins to change. A senior Siberian Husky usually exercises less, moves more slowly and sleeps more.

This change in your dog's lifestyle and physiological performance requires a change in diet. Because these changes take place slowly, they might not be recognizable at first. These metabolic changes increase the tendency toward obesity, requiring an even more vigilant approach to feeding. Obesity in an older dog exacerbates the health problems that already accompany old age.

As a Siberian ages, few of his organs will function up to par. The kidneys will slow down, and the intestines will become less efficient. These age-related factors are best handled with a change in diet and a change in feeding schedule to give smaller portions that are more easily digested.

There is no single best diet for an older Siberian Husky. While many older dogs will do perfectly fine on light or senior diets, other dogs will do better on special premium diets such as lamb and rice. Be sensitive to your senior Siberian Husky's diet, and this will help control other problems that may arise with your old friend.

Did You Know?

Because semimoist food contains lots of sugar, it isn't a good selection for your husky's main menu. However, it is great for an occasional yummy snack. Try forming into little meatballs for a once-a-week treat! She'll love ya for it!

These delicious, dog-friendly recipes will have your furry friend smacking her lips and salivating for more. Just remember: Treats aren't meant to replace your dog's regular meals. Give your Siberian snacks sparingly and continue to feed her nutritious, well-balanced meals.

Cheddar Squares

$1/3$ cup all-natural applesauce
$1/3$ cup low-fat cheddar cheese, shredded
$1/3$ cup water
2 cups unbleached white flour

In a medium bowl, mix all the wet ingredients. In a large bowl, mix all the dry ingredients. Slowly add all the wet ingredients to the dry mixture.

Mix well. Pour batter into a greased, 13x9x2-inch pan. Bake at 375-degrees Fahrenheit for 25 to 30 minutes. Bars are done when a toothpick inserted in the center and removed comes out clean. Cool and cut into bars. This recipe makes about 54, $1^{1}/_{2}$-inch bars.

Peanut Butter Bites

3 tablespoons vegetable oil
$1/4$ cup smooth peanut butter, no salt or sugar
$1/4$ cup honey
$1^{1}/_{2}$ teaspoon baking powder
2 eggs
2 cups whole wheat flour

In a large bowl, mix all ingredients until dough is firm. If the dough is too sticky, mix in a small amount of flour. Knead dough on a lightly floured surface until firm. Roll out dough half an inch thick, and cut with cookie cutters. Put cookies on a cookie sheet half an inch apart. Bake at 350-degrees Fahrenheit for 20 to 25 minutes. When done, cookies should be firm to the touch. Turn oven off and leave cookies for one to two hours to harden. This recipe makes about 40, 2-inch-long cookies.

HANDSOME

Like all the Northern breeds, the Siberian Husky is double-coated, with a downy coat next to the skin protected by a longer, stiffer guard coat. This soft, inner coat traps body heat while the outer guard coat keeps the heat from escaping as well as waterproofs the animal.

By nature, this dog is fastidiously clean and typically free from body odor and parasites. Like cats, Siberians seem to spend a lot of time licking and cleaning themselves. That said, you still will need to do some basic grooming to keep your Siberian looking tiptop.

GEAR UP

No matter what the commercials say, the ingredients you apply to your Siberian's coat will not change a brittle, lifeless coat into a soft, healthy one. The truth is that if you want your Siberian to have a healthy coat, then take a close look at your dog's diet. Healthy hair and skin begins with good nutrition. A good premium dog food is the best place to start nourishing a healthy coat. Your dog's diet is not the place to economize. Purchase the best food you can afford and

Did You Know? Nail clipping can be tricky, so many dog owners leave the task for the professionals. However, if you walk your dog on concrete, you may not have to worry about it. The concrete acts like a nail file and will help keep the nails neatly trimmed.

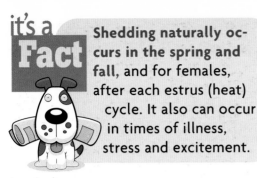

resist the impulse to save money at your Siberian's expense. Siberian Huskies' skin can be sensitive, so consult your veterinarian when selecting your dog's diet. Once you've established a complete and balanced diet, you can move on to improving the coat from the outside.

To keep your Siberian looking sharp, you will need a few grooming essentials:

- nail clippers
- styptic powder
- cotton balls – to put in your dog's ears when bathing
- a pH-balanced dog shampoo
- ear cleaner
- a coat conditioner
- a curved wire slicker brush – to remove shedding hair
- long-toothed rake
- double-sided stainless-steel comb
- a shedding rake – for peak shedding time

Like the metal-toothed slicker brush, the shedding blade must be used with caution. This dog's skin can easily be irritated by too heavy a touch or by using it in places where you shouldn't, such as against leg tendons or in such tender areas as the belly, genital or anal region.

BATH AND BRUSH

Unless your dog is sprayed by a skunk (in some grooming shops, curious Siberians hold the record for this one) or picks up a case of fleas, a bath every three months should suf-fice for this relatively odorless breed. Always make sure your dog's coat is thoroughly brushed out before bathing. Any mats or clumps of dead hair will only worsen when your dog gets wet.

The best place to bathe your husky is outside. Warm water will be more comfortable for him, and it will help loosen dead hair. If you choose to bathe him inside your house, place a nonskid mat in the tub and a strainer over the drain to catch hair. Also, Use a hand-held sprayer or cup.

Always check the water temperature before spraying your husky. Hold the hose or sprayer close to your Siberian Husky's body to avoid excessive spray. If you don't have a hose attachment, use a cup to scoop water and pour it over your dog.

Work from the highest to the lowest point with water and shampoo; use your fingers to massage the shampoo throughout the coat.

To keep water from getting into your dog's nose, hold your hand as a barrier around the nose, and let the water flow from behind his ears toward your hand.

Rinse your Siberian with a gentle flow of water until his coat feels clean and the water runs clear. You can use a coat conditioner after a bath, but use sparingly so as not to clog your dog's pores. Always follow the instructions on the bottle.

When drying your Siberian Husky's coat, use a blotting technique instead of rubbing the towel back and forth. If you use a hair dryer, test the air flow first, then hold it about 10 to 12 inches from your dog so you don't burn his skin. Professional groomers prefer air dryers that rely on velocity, not heat to protect a dog's sensitive skin.

Another brush-through and a spritz from a conditioning spray and your Siberian beauty is ready for anything.

NOTABLE & QUOTABLE

After removing a tick, clean your dog's skin with hydrogen peroxide. If Lyme disease is common where you live, have your veterinarian test the tick. Tick preventive medication will discourage ticks from attaching and kill any that do.

— groomer Andrea Vilardi from West Paterson, N.J.

NOW EAR THIS

Look way down inside your dog's ears. Do you see just a little tan wax? That's fine; leave it. Do you see gobs of gunk? That's not OK. If your Siberian is constantly scratching his ears and shaking his head, take a close look at that gunk. Place some on a piece of black paper and look at it with a magnifying glass. If you see little white moving specks, your dog has ear mites. You'll need a veterinarian to confirm your diagnosis, so that he or she can prescribe a proper and effective treatment that won't damage your dog's ears.

If your Siberian Husky tilts his head and acts like his ear hurts, or if the ear appears red and swollen, it's time to see the veterinarian. You don't want to clean his ears if he's in pain or if there's a chance of a perforated eardrum.

Assuming your Siberian Husky just has dirty ears, cleaning them is quite simple. Quickly squeeze some of the cleaning solution into your dog's ear; if you go slowly, the solution will tickle and he'll shake it right out. Keep your hand on the base of the ear, and massage the liquid in so it squishes all around. Your Siberian will shake the liquid out, flinging dissolved gunk all over the place, so you may want to do this outdoors.

Wipe clean any goop hanging on the ears with a cotton ball. For really dirty ears, do this several times in the course of a week.

Don't stick cotton swabs into your Siberian Husky's ears. They can irritate the skin, pack gunk more tightly or perforate the eardrum. Don't use powders, which will mix with the moisture and form a hard cake. Don't use hydrogen peroxide, which will leave the ear moist; and most of all, don't be overzealous in your cleaning. More problems are caused by owners stripping the ears of natural waxes than by neglecting to clean them.

Keep in mind that ear cleaning is only preventive care; it cannot cure an existing infection.

NAIL CLIPPING 4-1-1

The Siberian's feet are compact with tough, thick pads. To keep them this way, the nails must be kept short; if they grow too long, the foot can become splayed, ruining its neat catlike appearance and impeding the dog's fluid gait. As your puppy becomes accustomed to handling, clip his nails weekly. In the grooming shop, this job is made easier by placing the dog on a grooming table, but it can be performed on the floor as well.

Did You Know?

Much to their owners' chagrin, Siberians blow their coats twice a year, shedding their undercoats completely. This intense shedding period usually lasts for two or three weeks. Expect to be duly impressed by the amazing density and profusion of the Siberian coat as they repeatedly fill trash cans with armloads of that downy fluff. These dogs often appear to be molting when blowing coat; their hair comes out in tufts, usually beginning on the hind end and continuing forward on the body. If you choose to take your shedding husky to the groomer, after an initial brushing, a warm bath with a conditioning rinse will help loosen the hair and speed up the shedding process.

Puppies should be social-
ized to grooming tools and
techniques. That way, they
behave better when being
spruced up as an adult.

The best time to clip your dog's nails is immediately after a bath because the water will have softened the nails, and your Siberian may be somewhat tired-out. Nail trimming is recommended every two weeks, using nail clippers or a nail grinding tool.

Trimming nails are crucial to maintaining the Siberian Husky's normal foot shape. Long nails can permanently damage a dog's feet; the tight ligaments of round, arched feet will break down more quickly. If your dog's nails are clicking on the floor, they need trimming.

Your Siberian should be accustomed to having his nails trimmed at an early age because it will be part of your maintenance routine throughout his life. Not only do neatly trimmed nails look nicer, but long nails can unintentionally scratch someone. Also, long nails have a better chance of rip-

ping and bleeding, or causing your Siberian's toes to spread.

Before you start clipping, make sure you can identify the "quick" in each nail (the

Although the Siberian Husky is a low-maintenance breed when it comes to grooming, regular sessions are a great time to check for health issues such as bruises, bumps and scratches.

vein in the center of each nail). It will bleed if accidentally cut, which will be painful for your dog since it contains a web of nerve endings. Keep some type of clotting agent on hand, such as a styptic pencil or powder (the type used for shaving). This will quickly stop the bleeding when applied to the end of the cut nail. Do not panic if this happens, just stop the bleeding and talk soothingly to your dog. Once he has calmed down, move on to the next nail. It is better to clip a little at a time, particularly with dogs who have dark nails, where the quick isn't easily visible.

Hold your dog steady as you begin trimming his nails; you do not want him to make any sudden movements or try to run away. Talk to him calmly and stroke him as you trim. While holding his foot in your

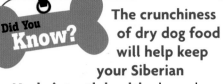
hand, simply take off the end of each nail in one quick clip. You can purchase nail clippers that are specifically made for dogs at pet-supply stores.

There are two predominant types of clippers. One is the guillotine clipper, which is a hole with a blade in the middle. Using this tool, squeeze the handles so that the blade meets the nail and chops it off. It sounds gruesome, and for some dogs, it is utterly intolerable. The second is the scissor-type clipper, which are gentler on the nail. The important thing to make sure of is that the blades on either of these clippers are sharp. Once the nails are at the desired length, use a nail file to smooth the rough edges of the nails so they don't catch on carpeting or outdoor debris.

A third option is a cordless nail grinder fitted with a fine grade (100 grit) sandpaper cylinder. Stone cylinders are more prone to heat buildup and vibration. When grinding, use a low-speed (5,000 to 10,000 rpm). Hold your dog's paw firmly in one hand spreading the toes slightly apart. Touch the spinning grinder wheel to the nail tip for one or two seconds without applying pressure. Repeat if necessary to remove the nail tip protruding beyond the quick. Grinders have the added benefit of leaving nails smooth and free of

Don't let your Siberian be embarrassed by his smile. Brush his teeth several times a week to keep his mouth healthy (and clean!).

sharp, jagged edges that traditional nail clippers leave behind.

If the procedure becomes more than you can deal with, remember: Groomers and vets charge a nominal fee to clip nails. By using their services you won't have to see your pet glower at you for the rest of the night.

When inspecting paws, you must check not only your dog's nails but also the pads of his paws. Check to see that the pads have not become cracked and always inspect between the pads to be sure nothing has become lodged there. Depending upon the season, there may be a danger of grass seeds or thorns becoming embedded, or even tar from the road. Butter, by the way, is useful in removing tar from your Siberian Husky's paws.

IT'S THE DARN TOOTH!

Like people, Siberian Huskies can suffer from dental disease, so experts recommend regular teeth cleanings. Daily brushing is best, but your dog will benefit from having his teeth brushed a few times a week. His teeth should be white and free of yellowish tartar, and his gums should appear healthy and pink. Gums that bleed easily when you perform dental duties may have gingivitis or some other dental disease. If this does occur, contact your veterinarian.

The first thing to know is that your puppy probably isn't going to want your fingers in his mouth. Desensitizing your puppy — getting him to accept that you will be looking at and touching his teeth — is the first step to overcoming his resistance. You can begin this as soon as you get your puppy, with the help of the thing that motivates dogs the most: food.

For starters, let your puppy lick some chicken, vegetable or beef broth off your finger. Then, dip your finger in broth again, and gently insert your finger in the side of your dog's mouth. Touch his side teeth and gums. Several sessions will get your puppy used to having his mouth touched.

Use a toothbrush specifically made for a dog or a fingertip brush to brush your Siberian Husky's teeth. Hold his mouth with one hand, and brush with the other. Use toothpaste formulated for dogs with delectable flavors like poultry and beef. Human toothpaste froths too much and can give your dog an upset stomach. Brush in a circular motion with the brush held at a 45-degree angle to the gum line. Be sure to get the fronts, tops and sides of each tooth.

Check the teeth for signs of plaque, tartar or gum disease, including redness, swelling, foul breath, discolored enamel near the gum line and receding gums. If you see these, immediately take your Siberian Husky to the veterinarian.

REWARD A JOB WELL DONE

Rewarding your Siberian Husky for behaving during grooming is the best way to ensure stress-free grooming throughout his lifetime. Bathing energizes your pet, and using the time immediately after grooming as play time is the best way to reward your husky for a job well done. Watching your clean, healthy Siberian tear from room to room in sheer joy is your reward for being a caring owner.

Give your husky treats for a good grooming session. Crunchy veggies like baby carrots are tasty and nutritious.

Every Siberian Husky deserves to look dapper. What do you need to keep your Siberian looking sharp? Go to Club Husky (**DogChannel.com/Club-Husky**) and download a checklist of essential grooming equipment you and your dog will need.

Six Tips for Husky Care

1. Grooming tools can be scary to some dogs, so let yours see and sniff everything at the start. Keep your beauty sessions short, too. Most huskies don't enjoy standing still for too long.
2. Look at your dog's eyes for any discharge, and her ears for inflammation, debris or foul odor. If you notice anything that doesn't look right, immediately contact your veterinarian.
3. Choose a time to groom your dog when you don't have to rush, and assemble all of the grooming tools before you begin. This way you can focus on your dog's needs instead of having to stop in the middle of the session to search for an item.
4. Start establishing a grooming routine the day after you bring her home. A regular grooming schedule will make it easier to remember what touch-up your dog needs.
5. Proper nail care helps with your dog's gait and spinal alignment. Nails that are too long can force a dog to walk improperly. Also, too-long nails can snag and tear, causing painful injury to your Siberian Husky.
6. Good dental health prevents gum disease and early tooth loss. Brush your Siberian's teeth daily and see a vet yearly for cleaning.

Six Questions to Ask a Groomer

1. Do you cage dry? Are you willing to hand dry or air dry my pet?
2. What type of shampoo are you using? Is it tearless? If not, do you have a tearless variety available for use?
3. Will you restrain my pet if she acts up during nail clipping? What methods do you use to handle difficult dogs?
4. Are you familiar with the Siberian Husky breed? Do you have any references from other Siberian owners?
5. Is the shop air-conditioned during hot weather?
6. Will my dog be getting brushed or just bathed?

TIME TO

TRAIN

Siberian Huskies are known all over the world as being friendly, playful dogs who make great family pets. Remember that the Chukchi people who originated the breed raised the dogs in a family atmosphere in the midst of their homes and with their children. The dogs grew up knowing that they were part of a family, just as your Siberian Husky will want to be an integral part of your family. The Siberian Husky will be loyal to those in his family, but he will still remain friendly to everyone he meets. In fact, a Siberian Husky can never have too many friends.

Huskies are also very tractable in that they had to be extremely amenable to discipline in order to perform their intended tasks. The sled driver had to have the utmost confidence in his dogs, since he depended on his dogs to be able to reliably scent a trail and find their way to food and back to the village. When man and dog are out on the frozen tundra, there are no signs to tell them which way to turn and no gas stations at which to stop for directions — getting lost in those conditions presents a

Did You Know?

The prime period for socialization is short. Most behavior experts agree that positive experiences during the 10-week period between 4 and 14 weeks of age are vital to the development of a puppy who'll grow into an adult dog with a sound temperament.

If your Siberian Husky refuses to sit with both haunches squarely beneath her and instead sits on one side or the other, she may have a physical reason for doing so. Discuss the habit with your veterinarian to be certain your dog isn't suffering from a structural problem.

life-threatening situation. Today, however, the most strenuous "food hunt" that the pet husky will probably engage in consists of something along the lines of a walk to the corner store with his owner, but trainability and dependability are still very much a part of the breed's character.

Siberian Huskies don't just take well to training; they require it. Huskies need discipline. A sled-dog driver had to rely on his dogs' ability to respond to his voice commands. These dogs had to be dependable (sometimes to a fault), especially the lead dog. Thus, huskies look to a leader to provide them with direction. As you know, the role of the leader is yours; it is your job to hold the reins!

The husky was bred first and foremost to be a working dog, and these working instincts are still a very large part of the dog's personality. Since the average pet husky owner will not be using his dog for hunting or pulling a sled, the dog needs to have his working energies redirected toward other activities. When not used in a working capacity, the Siberian Husky must have exercise or else he will be bored. A bored dog will find a way to amuse himself, which could spell trouble for your garden, furniture, shoes, etc. This is not to say that every dog will revert to destructive behavior when he has nothing else to do,

but wouldn't you rather be in control of how your dog spends his "free time?" Besides, occupying your dog's time gives you a chance to spend time together, constantly reinforcing the bond you formed when your Siberian Husky was just a pup.

CLICKER TRAINING

Reward-based training methods — clicking and luring — instruct dogs on what to do and help them do it correctly, setting them up for success and rewards rather than mistakes and punishment. A clicker is a small, plastic device that makes a sharp clicking sound when a button is pressed. You can purchase them at any pet-supply store.

Clicker training is a precise way to mark a desired behavior so an animal knows exactly what behavior earned the reward. Using a clicker, you "charge" the clicker by clicking

Your husky will look to you for guidance.

The best way to get your Siberian Husky well socialized is to introduce her to different kinds of people and situations. Have her meet a man with a beard, take her to a dog-friendly restaurant, take a ride in the car. Go online to download a socialization checklist at **DogChannel. com/Club-Husky**

JOIN OUR
ONLINE
Club
Husky™

and giving your Siberian Husky a treat several times, until he understands that the click means a treat is forthcoming. The click then becomes a secondary reinforcer. It's not the reward itself, but it will become so closely linked in your dog's mind with a reward that it has the same effect.

Next, you click the clicker when your Siberian Husky does any desirable behavior. Then, you follow it up with a click and treat. The click exactly marks, more precisely than a word or gesture, the desired behavior, quickly teaching your dog which behaviors will earn rewards.

Most dogs find food rewards meaningful; Siberian Huskies are no exception as they tend to be food-motivated. This works well because positive training relies on using treats, at least initially, to encourage a dog to demonstrate a certain behavior. The treat is then given as a reward. When you reinforce desired behaviors with rewards that are valuable to your dog, you are met with happy cooperation rather than resistance.

Positive reinforcement does not necessarily equal passivity. While you are rewarding your Siberian Husky's desirable behaviors, you must still manage him to be sure he isn't getting rewarded for his undesirable behaviors. Training tools, such as leashes, tethers, gates and crates, help keep your dog out of trouble. The use of force-free negative punishment (the dog's behavior makes a good thing go away) helps him realize there are negative consequences for inappropriate behaviors.

LEARNING SOCIAL GRACES

Now that you have done all of the preparatory work and have helped your Siberian Husky get accustomed to his new home and family, it's time for you to have some fun! Socializing your tiny pup gives you the opportunity to show off your new friend. Plus your Siberian Husky gets to reap the benefits of being an adorable little creature whom people will want to pet and gush over how precious he is.

Besides getting to know his new family, your puppy should be exposed to other people, animals and situations; but, of course, he must not come into close contact with dogs who you don't know well until he has had all his vaccinations. This will help him become well adjusted as he grows up and less prone to being timid or fearful of the new things he will encounter.

Your puppy's socialization began at the breeder's home, but now it is your responsibility to continue it. The socialization he receives up until he is 12 weeks of age is the most critical, as this is the time when he forms his impressions of the outside world. Be especially careful during the 8- to 10-week period, also known as the fear period. The interaction he receives during this time should be gentle and reassuring. Lack of socialization can manifest itself in fear and aggression as your Siberian Husky matures. Puppies require a lot of human contact, affection, handling and exposure to other animals.

Once your Siberian Husky has received his necessary vaccinations, feel free to take him out and about (on his leash, of course). Walk him around the neighborhood, take him on your daily errands, let people pet him and let him meet other dogs and pets. Make sure to expose your Siberian Husky to different people — men, women, kids, babies, men with beards, teenagers with cell phones or riding skateboards, joggers, shoppers, some- one in a wheelchair, a pregnant woman, etc. Make sure your Siberian Husky explores different surfaces like sidewalks, gravel and even a puddle. Positive experience is the key to building confidence. It's up to you to make sure your Siberian Husky safely discovers the world so he will be a calm, confident and well-socialized dog.

It's important that you take the lead in all socialization experiences and never put your

With the proper training, your Siberian will be as well behaved as she is adorable. One certification that all dogs should receive is the American Kennel Club Canine Good Citizen, which rewards dogs with good manners. Go to **DogChannel.com/Club-Husky** and click on "Downloads" to get the 10 steps required for your dog to be a CGC.

JOIN OUR
ONLINE
Club
Husky™

puppy in a scary or potentially harmful situation. Be mindful of your husky's limitations. Fifteen minutes at a public market is fine; two hours at a loud outdoor concert is too much. Meeting vaccinated, tolerant and gentle older dogs is great. Meeting dogs who you don't know or trust isn't a great idea, especially if they appear very energetic, dominant or fearful. Control the situations in which you place your puppy.

The best way to socialize your puppy to a new experience is to make him think it's the best thing ever. You can do this with a lot of happy talk, enthusiasm and, yes, food. To convince your puppy that almost any experience is a blast, always carry treats. Consider carrying two types — a bag of his puppy chow, which you can give him when introducing him to nonthreatening experiences, and a bag of high-value, mouth-watering treats to give him when introducing him to unfamiliar experiences.

BASIC CUES

All huskies, regardless of your training and relationship goals, need to know at least five basic good-manner behaviors: sit, down, stay, come and heel. Here are tips for teaching your Siberian these important cues.

SIT: Every dog should learn to sit.
- Hold a treat at the end of your Siberian Husky's nose
- Move the treat over his head.
- When your dog sits, click a clicker or say "Yes!"
- Feed your dog the treat.
- If your dog jumps up, hold the treat lower. If he backs up, back him into a corner and wait until he sits. Be patient. Keep your clicker handy, and click (or say "Yes!") and treat anytime he offers a sit.
- When he is able to easily offers sits, say "sit" just before he offers, so he can make the

SMART TIP!

If you begin teaching the heel cue by taking long walks and letting your dog pull you along, she may misinterpret this action as acceptable. When you pull back on the leash to counteract her pulling, she will read that tug as a signal to pull even harder!

association between the word and the behavior. Add the sit cue when you know you can get the behavior. He doesn't know what the word means until you repeatedly associate it with the appropriate behavior.
- When your Siberian Husky sits easily on cue, start using intermittent reinforcement by clicking some sits but not others. At first, click most sits and skip an occasional one (this is a high rate of reinforcement). Gradually make your clicks random.

DOWN: If your Siberian Husky can sit, then he can learn to lie down.
◆ Have your Siberian Husky sit.
◆ Hold the treat in front of his nose. Move it down slowly, straight toward the floor (toward his toes). If he follows all the way down, click and treat.
◆ If he gets stuck, move the treat down slowly. Click and treat for small movements downward — moving his head a bit lower, or inching one paw forward. Keep clicking and treating until your Siberian Husky is all the way down. This training method is called "shaping" — rewarding small pieces of a behavior until your dog succeeds.
◆ If your dog stands as you move the treat toward the floor, have him sit, and move the treat even more slowly downward, shaping with clicks and treats for small, downward movements. If he stands, cheerfully say "Oops!" (which means

"Sorry, no treat for that!"), have him sit and try again.

◆ If shaping isn't working, sit on the floor with your knee raised. Have your Siberian Husky sit next to you. Put your hand with the treat under your knee and lure him under your leg so he lies down and crawls to follow the treat. Click and treat!

◆ When you can lure the down easily, add the verbal cue, wait a few seconds to let your dog think, then lure him down to show him the association. Repeat until your dog goes down on the verbal cue; then begin using intermittent reinforcement.

STAY: What good are sit and down cues if your Siberian Husky doesn't stay?

▲ Start with your dog in a sit or down position.

▲ Put the treat in front of your dog's nose and keep it there.

▲ Click and reward several times while he is in position, then release him with a cue you will always use to tell him the stay is over. Common release cues are: "all done," "break," "free," "free dog," "at ease" and "OK."

▲ When your dog will stay in a sit or down position while you click and treat, add your verbal stay cue. Say "stay," pause for a second or two, click and say "stay" again. Release.

▲ When he is getting the idea, say "stay," whisk the treat out of sight behind your back, click the clicker and whisk the treat back. Be sure to get it all the way to his nose, so he doesn't jump up. Gradually increase the duration of the stay.

▲ When he will stay for 15 to 20 seconds, add small distractions: shuffling your feet, moving your arms, small hops. Gradually increase distractions. If your Siberian Husky makes mistakes, it means you're adding too much, too fast.

▲ When he'll stay for 15 to 20 seconds with distractions, gradually add distance. Have your Siberian Husky stay, take a half-step back, click, return and treat. When he'll stay with a half-step, tell him to stay,

Getting your dog's attention can be the most difficult part of training.

Once your husky understands what behavior goes with a specific cue, it is time to start weaning her off the food treats. At first, give a treat after each exercise. Then, start to give a treat only after every other exercise. Mix up times when you offer a food reward and when you only offer praise. This way your dog will never know when she is going to receive food and praise, or only praise.

take a full step back, click and return. Always return to your dog to treat after you click but before you release. If you always return, his stay becomes strong. If you call him to you, his stay gets weaker due to his eagerness to come to you.

COME: A reliable recall — coming when called — can be a challenging behavior to teach. It is possible, however. To succeed, you need to install an automatic response to your "come" cue — one so automatic that your Siberian Husky doesn't even stop to think when he hears it, but will spin on his heels and charge to you at full speed.

■ Start by charging a come cue the same way you charged your clicker. If your Siberian Husky already ignores the word "come," pick a different cue, like "front" or "hugs." Say your cue and feed him a bit of scrumptious treat. Repeat this until his eyes light up when he hears the cue. Now you're ready to start training.

■ With your Siberian Husky on a leash, run away several steps and cheerfully call out your charged cue. When he follows, click the clicker. Feed him a treat when he reaches you. For a more enthusiastic come, run away at full speed as you call him.

When he follows at a gallop, stop running, click and give him a treat. The better your Siberian Husky gets at coming, the farther away he can be when you call him.

■ Once your dog understands the come cue, play with more people, each holding a clicker and treats. Stand a short distance apart and take turns calling and running away. Click and treat in turn as he comes to each of you. Gradually increase the distance until he comes flying to each person from a distance.

■ When you and your Siberian Husky are ready to practice in wide-open spaces, attach a long line — a 20- to 50-foot leash — to your dog, so you can get a hold of him if that taunting squirrel nearby is too much of a temptation. Then, head to a practice area where there are less tempting distractions.

HEEL: Heeling means that your dog can calmly walk beside you without pulling. It takes time and patience on your part to succeed at teaching your dog that you will not proceed unless he is walking beside you with ease. Pulling out ahead on the leash is definitely unacceptable.

● Begin by holding the leash in your left hand as your Siberian Husky sits beside your left leg. Move the loop end of the leash to your right hand but keep your left hand short on the leash so it keeps your dog close to you.

● Say "heel" and step forward on your left foot. Keep your husky close to you and take three steps. Stop and have your dog sit next to you in what we now call the heel position. Praise verbally, but do not touch your dog. Hesitate a moment and begin again with "heel," taking three steps and stopping, at which point your dog is told to sit again.

Your goal here is to have your dog walk those three steps without pulling on the

If you want to make your dog happy, create a digging spot where she's allowed to disrupt the earth. Encourage her to dig there by burying bones and toys, and helping her dig them up. — Pat Miller, a certified dog trainer and owner of Peaceable Paws dog-training facility in Hagerstown, Md.

It's a good idea to enroll your Siberian Husky in an obedience class if one is available in your area. Many areas have dog clubs that offer basic obedience training and preparatory classes for obedience competition. There are also local dog trainers who offer similar classes.

leash. Once he will walk calmly beside you for three steps without pulling, increase the number of steps you take to five. When he will walk politely beside you while you take five steps, increase the length of your walk to 10 steps. Keep increasing the length of your stroll until your dog will walk beside you without pulling for as long as you want him to heel. When you stop heeling, indicate to the dog that the exercise is over by petting him and saying "OK, good dog." The "OK" is used as a release word, meaning that the exercise is finished, and he is free to relax.

● If you are dealing with a Siberian Husky who insists on pulling you around, simply put on your brakes and stand your ground until your husky realizes that the two of you are not going anywhere until he is beside you and moving at your pace, not his. It may take some time just standing there to convince your dog that you are the leader, and you will be the one to decide on the direction and speed of your travel.

● Each time your dog looks up at you or slows down to give a slack leash between the two of you, quietly praise him and say, "Good heel. Good dog." Eventually, your Siberian Husky will begin to respond, and within a few days he will be walking politely beside you without pulling on the leash. At first, the training sessions should be kept short and very positive; soon your Siberian Husky will be able to walk nicely with you for increasingly longer distances. Remember to give your Siberian Husky free time and the opportunity to run and play when you have finished heel practice.

TRAINING TIPS

If not properly socialized and trained, even a well-bred Siberian Husky will exhibit bad behaviors such as jumping up, barking, chasing, chewing and other destructive behaviors. You can prevent these habits and help your Siberian Husky become the perfect dog you've wished for by following some basic training and behavior guidelines.

Be consistent. Consistency is important, not just in terms of what you allow your Siberian to do (get on the sofa, perhaps) and not do (jump up on people), but also in the verbal and body language cues you use with your dog and in his daily routine.

Be gentle but firm. Positive training methods are very popular. Properly applied, dog-friendly methods are wonderfully effective, creating canine-human relationships based on respect and cooperation.

Manage behavior. All living things — especially dogs — repeat behaviors that are rewarded. Behaviors that aren't reinforced will go away.

Provide adequate exercise. A tired husky is a well-behaved husky. Many behavior problems can be avoided, others resolved, by providing your Siberian Husky with enough exercise.

THE THREE-STEP PROGRAM

Perhaps it's too late to give your dog consistency, training and management from the start. Maybe he came from a

Siberian Husky rescue shelter or you did not realize the importance of these basic guidelines when he was a puppy. He already may have learned some bad behaviors. Perhaps they're even part of his genetic package. Many problems can be modified with ease using the following three-step process for changing an unwanted behavior.

Step No. 1: Visualize the behavior you want your dog to exhibit. If you simply try to stop your Siberian Husky from doing something, you leave a behavior vacuum. You need to fill that vacuum with something, so your dog doesn't return to the same behavior or fill it with one that's even worse! If you're tired of your dog jumping up, decide what you'd prefer instead. A dog who greets people by sitting politely in front of them is a joy to own.

Step No. 2: Prevent your Siberian Husky from being rewarded for the behavior you don't want him to exhibit. Management to the rescue! When your Siberian Husky jumps up to greet you or get your attention, turn your back and step away to show him that jumping up no longer works in gaining your attention.

Step No. 3: Generously reinforce the desired behavior. Keep in mind that dogs will repeat behaviors that generate rewards. If your Siberian Husky no longer gets attention for jumping up and is heavily reinforced with attention and treats for sitting, he will offer sits instead of jumping,

because he's learned that sitting will get him what he wants.

COUNTER CONDITIONING

The three-step process helps to correct those behaviors that temporarily gives your Siberian Husky satisfaction. For example, he jumps up to get attention; he counter-surfs because he finds good food on coun-

ters; he nips at your hands to get you to play with him.

The three steps don't work well when you're dealing with behaviors that are based in strong emotion, such as aggression and fear, or with hardwired behaviors such as chasing prey. With these, you can change your dog's emotional or hardwired response through counter conditioning — programming a new emotional or automatic response to the stimulus by giving it a new association. Here's how you would counter condition a husky who chases after skateboarders while you're walking him on a leash.

1. Have a large supply of high-value treats, such as canned chicken.

2. Station yourself with your Siberian Husky on a leash at a location where skateboarders will pass by at a subthreshold distance "X" — that is, where your Siberian Husky is alerted to the approaching person but doesn't bark.

3. Wait for a skateboarder. The instant your Siberian Husky notices the skateboarder, feed him bits of chicken, nonstop, until the skateboarder is gone. Stop feeding him.

4. Repeat many times until, when the skateboarder appears, your Siberian Husky looks at you with a big grin as if to say, "Yay! Where's my chicken?" This is a conditioned emotional response, or CER.

5. When you have a consistent CER at distance X, decrease the distance slightly, perhaps minus 1 foot, and repeat until you consistently get the CER at this distance.

6. Continue decreasing the distance and obtaining a CER at each level, until a skateboarder zooming right past your Siberian Husky elicits the "Where's my chicken?" response. Now go back to distance X and add a second skateboarder. Continue this process of desensitization until your Siberian Husky doesn't turn a hair at a bevy of skateboarders.

LEAVE IT ALONE

Siberian Huskies enjoy eating, which makes it easy to train them using treats. But there's a downside to their gastronomic gusto; some Siberian Huskies will gobble down anything even remotely edible. This could include fresh food, rotten food, things that once were food and any item that's ever been in contact with food. So, if you don't want your Siberian Husky gulping trash, teach him to leave things alone when told.

Place a tempting tidbit on the floor and cover it with your hand (gloved against teeth, if necessary). Say your cue word ("leave it" or "nah"). Your dog might lick, nibble and paw your hand; don't give in or you'll be rewarding bad manners.

Wait until he moves away, then click or praise, and give a treat. Do not let your dog eat the food that's on the floor, only the treats you give him. Repeat until your Siberian Husky stops moving toward the tempting food.

Lift your hand momentarily, letting your dog see the temptation. Say the cue word.

Be ready to protect the treat but instantly reward him if he resists temptation. Repeat, moving your hand farther away and waiting longer before clicking and rewarding.

Increase the difficulty gradually — practice in different locations, add new temptations, drop treats from standing height, drop several at a time and step away.

Remember to use your cue word, so your Siberian Husky will know what he's expected to do. Always reward good behavior! Rehearse this skill daily for a week. After that, you'll have enough real-life opportunities to practice.

Teaching the down cue is easy once you have mastered the sit cue

BAD BEHAVIOR

iscipline — training one to act in accordance with rules — brings order to life. It is as simple as that. Without discipline, particularly in a group society, chaos reigns supreme and the group will eventually perish. Humans and canines are social animals and need some form of discipline in order to function effectively. Dogs need discipline in their lives in order to understand how their pack (you and other family members) functions and how they must act in order to survive.

Living with an untrained husky is like owning a piano that you do not know how to play; it is a nice object to look at but it does not do much more than that to bring you pleasure. Now, try taking piano lessons and suddenly the piano comes alive and brings forth magical sounds and rhythms that set your heart singing and your body swaying.

The same is true of your Siberian. Every dog is a big responsibility, and if not sensibly trained may develop unacceptable behaviors that annoy you or cause family friction.

To begin to train your Siberian Husky, enroll him in an obedience class to teach him good manners as you learn how and why he behaves the way he does. You will also find out how to communicate with your Siberian Husky and how to recognize and understand his communications with you. Suddenly your dog will take on a new role in your life; he will be interesting, smart, well behaved and fun to be with. He will demonstrate his bond of devotion to you daily. In other words, your Siberian Husky will do wonders for your ego because he will constantly remind you that you are not only his leader, you are his hero!

Those involved with teaching dog obedience and counseling owners about their dogs' behavior have discovered interesting facts about dog ownership. For example, training dogs when they are puppies results in the highest success rate in developing well-mannered and well-adjusted adults. Training an older Siberian, from 6 months to 6 years, can produce almost equal results, providing that the owner accepts the dog's slower learning rate and is willing to patiently work to help him succeed. Unfortunately, many owners of untrained adult dogs lack the necessary patience, so they do not persist until their dogs are successful at learning particular behaviors.

Training a 10- to 16-week-old Siberian Husky puppy (20 weeks maximum) is like working with a dry sponge in a pool of water. The pup soaks up whatever you teach him and constantly looks for more to do and learn. At this early age, his body is not yet producing hormones, and therein lies the reason for such a high success rate.

Did You Know?

Anxiety can make a pup miserable. Living in a world with scary monsters and suspected husky-eaters roaming the streets has to be pretty nerve wracking. The good news is that timid dogs are not doomed to be forever ruled by fear. Owners who understand a timid Siberian Husky's needs can help her build self-confidence and a more optimistic view of life.

Without hormones, he is focused on you and is not particularly interested in investigating other places, dogs, people, etc.

You are his leader; his provider of food, water, shelter and security. Your puppy latches onto you and wants to stay close. He will usually follow you from room to room, won't let you out of his sight when you are outdoors with him and will respond in like manner to the people and animals you encounter. If you greet a friend warmly, he will happily greet the person as well. If, however, you are hesitant, even anxious, about the approaching stranger, he will also respond accordingly.

Once your Siberian Husky puppy begins to produce hormones, his natural curiosity will emerge, and he will begin to investigate the world around him. It is at this time when you may notice your untrained dog begins to wander and ignore your cues to stay close.

SMART TIP!

The golden rule of dog training is simple. For each "question" (cue), there is only one correct "answer" (reaction). One cue equals one reaction. Keep practicing the cue until the dog reacts correctly without hesitation. Be repetitive but not monotonous. Dogs get bored just as people do; a bored dog's attention will not be focused on the lesson.

There are usually training classes within a reasonable distance of your home, but you also can do a lot to train your dog yourself. Sometimes classes are available but the tuition is too costly, whatever the circumstances, information about training your Siberian Husky without formal obedience classes lies within the pages of this book. If the recommended procedures are

The best way to get through to dogs is through their stomach and mind — not the use of force. You have to play a mind game with them.

— *Sara Gregware, a professional dog handler and trainer in Goshen, Conn.*

followed faithfully, you can expect positive results that will prove rewarding for both you and your dog.

Whether your Siberian Husky is a puppy or a mature adult, the teaching methods and training techniques used in basic behaviors are the same. No dog, whether puppy or adult, likes harsh or inhumane training methods. All creatures, however, respond favorably to gentle motivational methods and sincere praise and encouragement.

The following behavioral issues are those most commonly encountered. Remember, every dog and situation is unique. Because behavioral abnormalities are the leading reason for owners' abandoning their pets, we hope that you will make a valiant effort to solve your husky's behavioral issues.

NIP NIPPING

As puppies start to teethe, they feel the need to sink their teeth into anything — unfortunately that includes your fingers, arms, hair, toes, whatever happens to be available. You may find this behavior cute for about the first five seconds — until you feel just how sharp those puppy teeth are.

Nipping is something you want to discourage immediately and consistently with a firm "No!" (or whatever number of firm "nos" it takes for your dog to understand that you mean business) and replace your finger with an appropriate chew toy.

STOP THAT WHINING

A puppy will often cry, whine, whimper, howl or make some type of commotion when he is left alone. This is basically his way of calling out for attention, of calling out to make sure that you know he is there and that you have not forgotten about him. He feels insecure when he is left alone; for example, when you are out of the house and he is in his crate, or when you are in another part of the house and he cannot see you.

The noise he is making is an expression of the anxiety he feels at being alone, so he needs to be taught that being alone is OK. You are not actually training your Siberian Husky to stop making noise, you are training him to feel comfortable when he is alone and thus removing the need to make the noise.

This is where his crate with a cozy blanket and a toy comes in handy. You want to know that your pup is safe when you are not there to supervise, so the best place for him to be is in his crate, rather than roaming about the house. In order for your pup to stay in his crate without making a fuss, he needs to be comfortable there. It is extremely important that your dog's crate is never used as a form of punishment, or your Siberian Husky puppy will have a negative association with his crate.

Accustom your puppy to his crate in short, gradually increasing time intervals. During these periods, put him in the crate, maybe with a treat, and stay in the room with him. If he cries or makes a fuss, do not go to him, but stay in his sight. Gradually, he will realize staying in his crate is all right without your help and it will not be so traumatic for him when you are not around. You may want to leave the radio on softly when you leave the house; the sound of human voices can comfort him.

Your Siberian Husky may howl, whine or otherwise vocalize her displeasure at your leaving the house and her being left alone. This is a normal case of separation anxiety, but there are things that can be done to eliminate this problem. Your dog needs to learn that she will be fine on her own for a while and that she will not wither away if she isn't attended to every minute of the day.

In fact, constant attention can lead to separation anxiety in the first place. If you are endlessly coddling and cuddling your husky, she will come to expect this from you all of the time, and it will be more traumatic for her when you are not there.

To help minimize separation anxiety, make your entrances and exits as low-key as possible. Do not give your husky a long, drawn-out goodbye, and do not lavish her with hugs and kisses when you return. This will only make her miss you more when you are away. Another thing you can try is to give your dog a treat when you leave; this will keep her occupied, keep her mind off the fact that you just left and help her associate your leaving with a pleasant experience.

You may have to acclimate your husky to being left alone in intervals, much like when you introduced her to her crate. Of course, when your dog starts whimpering as you approach the door, your first instinct will be to run to her and comfort her, but don't do it! Eventually, she will adjust and be just fine — if you take it in small steps. Her anxiety stems from being placed in an unfamiliar situation; by familiarizing her with being alone, she will learn that she will be just fine.

When your Siberian Husky is alone in the house, confine her in her crate or other designated dog-proof area. This should be the area in which she sleeps, so she will already feel comfortable there and this should make her feel more at ease when she is alone. This is just one of the many examples in which a crate is an invaluable tool for you and your Siberian Husky, and another reinforcement of why your dog should view her crate as a happy place of her own.

Do not carry your puppy to her potty area. Lead her there on a leash or, better yet, encourage her to follow you to the spot. If you start carrying her, you might end up doing this routine for a long time, and your puppy will have the satisfaction of having trained you.

CHEW ON THIS

The national canine pastime is chewing! Every dog loves to sink his "canines" into a tasty bone, but anything will do! Dogs chew to massage their gums, make their new teeth feel better and exercise their jaws. This is a natural behavior deeply imbedded in all things canine. Owners should not stop their dog's chewing, but redirect it to chewworthy objects. A smart owner will purchase proper chew toys for their Siberian Husky, like strong nylon bones made for large dogs. Be sure that these devices are safe and durable because your dog's safety is at risk.

The best solution is prevention: That is, put your shoes, handbags and other alluring objects in their proper places (out of the reach of the growing canine mouth). Direct puppies to their toys whenever you see them tasting the furniture legs or the leg of your pants. Make a loud noise to attract your Siberian Husky pup's attention and immediately escort him to his chew toy and engage him with the toy for at least four minutes, praising and encouraging him all the while.

NO MORE JUMPING

Jumping is a dog's friendly way of saying hello! Some owners don't mind when their dog jumps, which is fine for them. The problem arises when guests arrive and the dog greets them in the same manner — whether they like it or not! However friendly the greeting is intended to be, chances are your visitors will not appreciate your dog's enthusiasm. Your dog will not be able to distinguish upon whom he can jump and whom he cannot. Therefore, it is probably best to discourage this behavior entirely.

Pick a cue such as "off" (avoid using "down" because you will use that for your dog to lie down) and tell him "off" when he jumps. Place him on the ground on all fours and have him sit, praising him the whole time. Always lavish him with praise and petting when he is in the sit position, that way you are still giving him a warm, affectionate greeting, because you are as pleased to see him as he is to see you!

UNWANTED BARKING MUST GO

Barking is how dogs talk. It can be somewhat frustrating because it is not always easy to tell what your dog means by his bark: Is he excited, happy, frightened, angry? Whatever it is he is trying to say, he should not be punished for barking. It is only when barking becomes excessive, and when excessive barking becomes a bad habit, that the behavior needs to be modified.

If an intruder came into your home in the middle of the night and your dog barked a warning, wouldn't you be pleased? You would probably deem your dog a hero, a wonderful guardian and protector of the home. On the other hand, if a friend unexpectedly drops by, rings the doorbell and is greeted with a sudden sharp bark, you would probably be annoyed at your dog. But isn't it the same behavior? Your dog doesn't know any better … unless he sees who is at the door and it is someone he is familiar with, he will bark as a means of vocalizing that his (and your) territory is being threatened. While your friend is not posing a

Dogs bark; that's what they do. A dog who barks constantly needs to be taught when it is appropriate to be quiet.

threat, it is all the same to your dog. Barking is his means of letting you know there is an intruder, whether friend or foe, on your property. This type of barking is instinctive and should not be discouraged.

Excessive, habitual barking, however, is a problem that should be corrected early on. As your Siberian Husky grows up, you will be able to tell when his barking is purposeful and when it is for no reason; you will able to distinguish your dog's different barks and with what they are associated. For example, the bark when someone comes to the door will be different from the bark when he is excited to see you. It is similar to a person's tone of voice, except that your Siberian Husky has to completely rely on tone because he does not have the benefit of using words. An incessant barker will be evident at an early age.

There are some things that encourage barking. For example, if your Siberian Husky barks nonstop for a few minutes and you give him a treat to quiet him, he

Stage false departures. Pick up your car keys and put on your coat, then put them away and go about your routine. Do this several times a day, ignoring your dog while you do it. Soon, her reaction to these triggers will decrease.

— *September Morn, a dog trainer and behavior specialist in Bellingham, Wash.*

believes you are rewarding him for barking. He will now associate barking with getting a treat and will keep barking until he receives his reward.

FOOD STEALING AND BEGGING

Is your Siberian Husky devising ways of stealing food from your cupboards? If so, you must answer the following questions: Is your dog really hungry? Why is there food on the coffee table? Face it: Some dogs are more food-motivated than others; some are totally obsessed by a slab of brisket and can only think of their next meal. Food stealing is terrific fun and always yields a great reward — food, glorious food!

Therefore, a smart owner's goal is to make the reward less rewarding, even startling! Plant a shaker can (an empty can with a lid filled with coins) on the table so that it catches your pooch off-guard. There are other devices available that will surprise your dog when he is looking for a mid-afternoon snack. Such remote-control devices, though not the first choice of some trainers, allow the correction to come from the object instead of you. These devices are also useful to keep your snacking Siberian Husky from napping on forbidden furniture.

Just like food stealing, begging is a favorite pastime of hungry pups with the same reward — food! Dogs learn quickly that humans love that feed-me pose and that their owners keep the good food for themselves. Why would humans dine on kibble when they can cook up sausages and kielbasa? Begging is a conditioned response related to a specific stimulus, time and place; the sounds of the kitchen, cans and bottles opening, crinkling bags and the smell of food preparation will excite your chowhound and soon his paws are in the air!

Here is how to stop this behavior: Never give in to a beggar, no matter how appealing or desperate! By giving in, you are rewarding your dog for jumping up, whining and rubbing his nose into you. By ignoring your dog, you eventually will force the behavior into extinction. Note that his behavior will likely get worse before it disappears, so be sure there are not any softies in the family who will give in to your Siberian Husky every time he whimpers "Please."

DIG THIS

Digging, seen as a destructive behavior by humans, is actually quite a natural behavior in dogs. Their desire to dig can be irrepressible and most frustrating. When digging happens, it is an innate behavior redirected into something the dog can do in his everyday life. In the wild, a dog would be actively seeking food, making his own shelter, etc. He would be using his paws in a purposeful manner for his survival. Because you provide him with food and shelter, he has no need to use his paws for these purposes and so the energy he would be using may manifest itself in the form of holes all over your yard and flower beds.

Perhaps your dog is digging as a reaction to boredom — it is somewhat similar to someone eating a whole bag of chips in front of the TV — because they are there and there is nothing better to do! Basically, the answer is to provide your dog with adequate play and exercise so his mind and paws are occupied, and so he feels as if he is doing something useful.

Of course, digging is easiest to control if it is stopped as soon as possible, but it is often hard to catch your dog in the act. If your Siberian Husky is a compulsive digger and is not easily distracted by other activities, you can designate an area on your property where it is OK for him to dig. If you catch him digging in an off-limits area of the yard, immediately bring him to the approved area and praise him for digging there. Keep a close eye on him so you can catch him in the act — that is the only way to make him understand where digging is permitted and where it is not. If you take him to a hole he dug an hour ago and tell him "no," he will understand that you are not fond of holes, dirt or flowers. If you catch him while he is stifle-deep in your tulips, that is when he will get your message.

POOP ALERT!

Humans find feces eating, aka *coprophagia*, one of the most disgusting behaviors that their dog could engage in; yet to your dog it is perfectly normal. Vets have found that diets with low digestibility, containing relatively low levels of fiber and high levels of starch, increase *coprophagia*. Therefore, high-fiber diets may decrease the likelihood

Many behavior problems can be remedied with basic cues such as sit, down and stay.

of your dog eating feces. To discourage this behavior, feed nutritionally complete food in the proper amount. If changes in his diet do not seem to work, and no medical cause can be found, you will have to modify his behavior through environmental control before it becomes a habit.

There are some tricks you can try, such as adding an unpleasant-tasting substance to the feces to make them unpalatable or adding something to your dog's food which will make it unpleasant tasting after it passes through your dog. The best way to prevent your dog from eating his stool is to make it unavailable — clean up after he eliminates and remove any stool from the yard. If it is not there, he cannot eat it.

Never reprimand your dog for stool eating, as this rarely impresses your dog. Vets recommend distracting your Siberian Husky while he is in the act. Another option is to muzzle your dog when he goes in the yard to relieve himself; this usually is effective within 30 to 60 days. *Coprophagia* is mostly seen in pups 6 to 12 months and usually disappears around the dog's first birthday.

AGGRESSION

Aggression, when not controlled, always becomes dangerous. An aggressive Siberian Husky, may lunge at, bite or even attack a person or other dog. Aggressive behavior is not to be tolerated. It is more than just inappropriate behavior; it is not safe. It is painful for a family to watch their dog become unpredictable in his behavior to the point where they are afraid of him. While not all aggressive behavior is dangerous, growling and baring teeth can be frightening. It is important to ascertain why your dog is acting in this manner. Aggression is a display of dominance, and your dog should not have the dominant role in his pack, which is, in this case, your family.

It is important not to challenge an aggressive dog, as this could provoke an attack. Observe your Siberian Husky's body language. Does he make direct eye contact and stare? Does he try to make himself as large as possible: ears pricked, chest out, neck arched? Height and size signify authority in a dog pack — being taller or "above" another dog literally means that he is "above" in the social status. These body signals tell you that your Siberian Husky thinks he is in charge, a problem that needs to be addressed. An aggressive dog is unpredictable: You never know when he is going to strike and what he is going to do. You cannot understand why a dog that is playful and loving one minute is growling and snapping the next.

The best solution is to consult a behavioral specialist, one who has experience with Siberian Huskies if possible. Together, perhaps you can pinpoint the cause of your dog's aggression and do something about it. An aggressive dog cannot be trusted and a dog who cannot be trusted is not safe to have as a family pet. If, very unusually, you find that your dog has become untrustworthy and you feel it necessary to seek a new home with a more suitable family and environment, explain fully to the new owners all your reasons for rehoming the dog to be fair

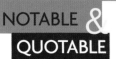
The purpose of puppy classes is for puppies to learn how to learn. The pups get the training along the way, but the training is almost secondary.

— professional trainer Peggy Shunick Duezabou of Helena, Mont.

to all concerned. In the very worst case, you will have to consider euthanasia.

AGGRESSION TOWARD DOGS

A dog's aggressive behavior toward another dog sometimes stems from insufficient exposure to other dogs at an early age. In Siberian Huskies, early socialization with other dogs is essential.

It is the breeder and owner's responsibility to curb and redirect any signs of aggression so that your Siberian Husky can become an upright member of canine society. If other dogs make your Siberian Husky nervous and agitated, he might use aggression as a defensive mechanism. A dog who has not received sufficient exposure to other canines tends to believe he is the only dog on the planet. He then becomes so dominant that he does not even show signs that he is fearful or threatened. Without growling or any other physical warning sign, he will lunge at and bite another dog. A way to correct this is to let your Siberian Husky approach another dog only when walking on a leash. Watch very closely and at the very first sign of aggression, correct your dog and pull him away. Scold him for any sign of discomfort, and praise him when he ignores or tolerates the other dog. Keep this up until he stops the aggressive behavior, learns to ignore other dogs or accepts other dogs. Always praise him lavishly for his correct behavior.

DOMINANT AGGRESSION

A social hierarchy is firmly established in a wild dog pack; dogs want to dominate those under him and please those above him. They know there must be a leader. If you are not the obvious choice for emperor, your dog will assume the throne! These conflicting, innate desires are what you are up against when training your dog. In training a dog to obey cues, you are reinforcing the fact that you are the top dog in the "pack" and that your dog should, and should want to, serve his superior. Thus, you are suppressing your dog's urge to dominate by modifying his behavior and making him obedient.

An important part of training is taking every opportunity to reinforce that you are the leader. The simple action of making your Siberian Husky sit to wait for his food says you control when he eats and that he is dependent on you for food. Although it may be difficult, do not give in to your dog's wishes every time he whines at you or looks at you with his pleading eyes. It is a constant effort to show your dog that his place in the pack is at the bottom. This is not meant to sound cruel or inhumane. You love your Siberian Husky and you should treat him with care and affection. You certainly did not get a dog just so you could boss around another creature. Dog training is not about being cruel or feeling important, it is about molding your dog's behavior into what is acceptable and teaching him to live by your rules. In theory, it is quite simple: Catch him in appropriate behavior and reward him for it. Add a dog into the equation and it becomes a bit more trying, but as a rule of thumb, positive reinforcement works best.

With a dominant dog, punishment and negative reinforcement can have the opposite effect of what you are trying to achieve. It can make your dog fearful and/or act out aggressively if he feels he is being challenged. Remember, a dominant dog perceives himself at the top of the social heap and will fight to defend his perceived status. The best way to prevent that is to never give him reason to think he is in control in the first place. If you are having trouble training your Siberian Husky and it seems as if he is constantly challenging your authority, seek the help of an obedience trainer or behavioral specialist. A professional will work with both you and your dog to teach you effective techniques to use at home. Beware of trainers who rely on excessively harsh methods; scolding is necessary now and then, but the focus in your training should always be positive reinforcement.

If you can isolate what brings out your Siberian Husky's fear reaction, you can help him get over it. Supervise your Siberian Husky's interactions with people and other dogs, and praise him when it goes well. If he starts to act aggressively in a situation, correct him and remove him from the situation. Do not let people approach your dog and start petting him without your expressed permission. That way, you can have your dog sit to accept petting and praise him when he behaves appropriately; you are focusing on praise and modifying his behavior by rewarding him. By being gentle and by supervising his interactions, you are showing him that there is no need to be afraid or defensive.

SEXUAL BEHAVIOR

Dogs exhibit certain sexual behaviors that may have influenced your choice of male or female when you first purchased your Siberian Husky. To a certain extent, spaying/neutering will eliminate these behaviors, but if you are purchasing a dog that you wish to breed, you should be aware of what you will have to deal with throughout your dog's life.

Female dogs usually have two estruses per year with each season lasting about three weeks. These are the only times in which a female dog will mate, and she usually will not allow this until the second week of the cycle, but this does vary from female to female. If not bred during the heat cycle, it is not uncommon for a female to experience a false pregnancy, in which her mammary glands swell and she exhibits maternal tendencies toward toys or other objects.

Smart dog owners must also recognize that mounting is not merely a sexual expression. It is also one of dominance. Be consistent and persistent in your training, and you will find that you can move mounters."

One of the best ways to nurture a cooperative and solid relationship with your Siberian Husky is to become involved in an activity both of you can enjoy. A bored Siberian Husky can easily become a troublesome dog.

Deciding what recreation activity you and your Siberian Husky would enjoy the most takes some consideration. Do you want a sport, such as agility, where you and your dog are both active participants? Would you prefer an activity, such as flyball, where your dog does most of the work? Does something less physical, such as visiting senior citizens, sound more like your cup of tea? Perhaps a brief synopsis of some of the more popular dog-friendly recreations will help you narrow down the choices.

EXERCISE OPTIONS

All Siberian Huskies need exercise to keep them physically and mentally healthy. An inactive dog is an overweight dog, who will likely suffer joint strain or torn ligaments. Inactive dogs also are prone to mischief and may do anything to relieve their boredom. This often leads to behavioral problems, such as chewing or barking. Regular daily exercise, such as walks and play sessions, will keep your Siberian Husky slim, trim and happy.

Did You Know? The Fédération Internationale Cynologique is the world kennel club that governs dog shows in Europe and elsewhere around the world.

Provide your Siberian Husky with interactive play that stimulates his mind as well as his body. It's a good idea to have a daily period of one-on-one play, especially with a puppy or young dog. Continue this type of interaction throughout your dog's life, and you will build a lasting bond. Even senior Siberian Huskies need the stimulation that activity provides.

If your Siberian Husky is older or overweight, consult your veterinarian about how much and what type of exercise he needs. Usually, a 10- to 15-minute walk once a day is a good start. As the pounds start to drop off, your dog's energy level will rise, and you can increase the amount of daily exercise.

Whether a dog is trained in the structured environment of a class or alone with his owner at home, there also are many sporting activities that can bring fun and rewards to owner and dog once they have mastered basic training techniques.

AGILITY TRIALS

Agility is a fast-growing sport, attracting dogs of all kinds and their equally diverse owners. In agility, the dog, off leash but guided by the handler, runs a course of obstacles including jumps, tunnels, A-frames, elevated boards called dog walks and more. Basically, the dog must negotiate the obstacles in proper order and style and do it within a set time. The team can strive for high honors, the titles only or simply for the joy of working together.

Most training facilities require that dogs have some basic obedience before entering an agility class because your dog must be responsive to you and reliable about not interfering with other dogs and handlers or running off. It is also important to allow your puppy to mature before undertaking agility's jumps and sharp turns because young bones

Before You Begin:
Because of the physical demands of sporting activities, a Siberian Husky puppy shouldn't begin official training until she is done growing. That doesn't mean, though, that you can't begin socializing her to sports. Talk to your veterinarian about what age is appropriate to begin.

and joints are injured more easily than mature ones.

Multiple organizations sponsor agility titles at all levels, from novice to advanced. The rules, procedures and obstacles vary among the organizations, so, again, it's important to obtain and read the appropriate rule book before entering your dog in competition. In addition to the American Kennel Club and United Kennel Club, the United States Dog Agility Association and the North American Dog Agility Council also offer agility trials and titles.

The AKC offers Novice Agility, Open Agility, Agility Excellent and Master Agility Excellent titles. To achieve an MX title, a dog must first earn the AX title, then earn qualifying scores in the agility excellent class at 10 licensed or member agility trials.

The USDAA offers eight agility titles. An Agility Dog has achieved three clear rounds (no faults) under two different judges in the starters or novice category of competition. An Advanced Agility Dog has achieved three clear rounds under two different judges in the Advanced class. The Masters Agility Dog has demonstrated versatility by achieving three clear rounds under two different judges in the masters standard agility class.

In addition, a dog must receive a qualifying score at the masters level in each of the following: Gamblers Competition, to demonstrate proficiency in distance control and handling; Pairs or Team Relay, to demonstrate cooperative team effort and good sportsmanship; Jumping Class, to demonstrate jumping ability and fluid working habit; and Snooker Competition, to further demonstrate a dog and handler's versatility in strategic planning. To earn a Jumpers Master, Gamblers Master, Snooker Master or Relay Master title, a dog must achieve five clear rounds in the appropriate class. A USDAA Agility Dog Champion (ADCh.) has earned the MAD, SM, GM, JM and RM titles. The USDAA also recognizes the Agility Top 10 annually.

USDAA promotes competition by hosting major tournament events, including its Grand Prix of Dog Agility championships. The Dog Agility Masters Team Pentathlon Championship promotes agility as a team sport, and the Dog Agility Steeplechase championship focuses on speed in performance. Dogs must be registered with the USDAA in order to compete in its events.

The USDAA also offers programs for older dogs and younger handlers. The Veterans Program is for dogs 7 years of age or older. The Junior Handler Program is for handlers up to 18 years of age and is designed to encourage young people to participate in dog agility as a fun, recreational family sport.

The North American Dog Agility Council offers certificates of achievement for the regular, jumpers and gamblers classes. The purpose of the regular agility class is to demonstrate the handler and dog's ability to perform all of the agility obstacles safely and at a moderate rate of speed.

At the open level, the goal is to test the handler and dog's ability to perform the obstacles more quickly and with more

Agility has plenty of fun obstacles — from jumps to tunnels to turns to hoops — that are sure to keep your Siberian enthused.

Sports are physically demanding. Have your vet perform a full examination of your Siberian to rule out joint problems, heart disease, eye ailments and other maladies. Once you get the green light, start having fun in your new dog-sporting life!

directional and distance control and obstacle discrimination.

At the elite level, more complex handler strategies are tested, with the dog moving at a brisk pace. The dog may be entered in the standard, veterans or junior handlers division. In all divisions, certification in the regular agility classes will require three qualifying rounds under at least two different judges. NADAC also awards the Agility Trial Champion title.

THE ORIGINAL SIBERIAN SPORT

Siberian Huskies originated in Siberia with the Chukchi people, who needed a dog who could work hard and survive in the frigid climate. Although Siberian Huskies can be found all over the world today, in a variety of climates, these dogs still enjoy the cold and snow. If you live in a region where snow is a regular visitor each winter, there are several sports you can enjoy with your dog.

Sledding is not a sport for an owner who has just one dog, however. The minimum size for most recreational husky teams is usually four dogs. But even that might not be enough. If one dog is sore or is hurt, then the entire team is out of action.

Sledding also requires an investment in equipment and that can be expensive for a beginner. One harness usually costs $20 to $25, plus $500 or more for a basic sled. You will also need traces (the lines that connect your dog to the sled), as well as booties for the dog (to prevent ice and snow cuts to the pads). Some dogs also need padding under the harness. A wheeled cart is usually a good idea to increase the team's fitness level prior to the arrival of snow. This can be another $500 investment.

"Dog sledding is my favorite sport because it lets me get out with my dogs doing what they were bred to do," says Sheila Blanker, a veterinarian in Northfield, Mass., and representative for the Siberian Husky Club of America's Working Pack Dog Program. "I have seen more wildlife and animal tracks, and experienced a lot from the back of a sled."

For more information about sledding, the sport and the equipment you will need to participate, visit www.sleddogcentral. com. Becoming more familiar with the sport prior to investing a great deal of money into it is a good idea. Sled Dog Central also offers a mentoring program so that beginners can be guided through the process of getting started.

Read about the similar sports of carting, skijorning and skatejorning on page 159.

OBEDIENCE TRIALS

Obedience trials in the United States trace back to the early 1930s, when organized obedience training was developed to demonstrate how well dogs and their owners could work together. Helen Whitehouse Walker, a Standard Poodle fancier, pioneered obedience trials after she modeled a series of exercises after the Associated Sheep, Police and Army Dog Society of Great Britain. Since Walker initiated the first trials, competitive obedience has grown by leaps and bounds, and today more than 2,000 trials are held in the

More Sports

Pulling a sled was the original sport for Siberian Huskies, but it's not the only one that they can participate in today. All of these require a good foundation of obedience training prior to beginning training.

Flyball: Furiously fast, this relay race consists of a box loaded with tennis balls that ejects a ball whenever a dog jumps against the release. Four hurdles, set at a height appropriate for the shortest canine on the team of four, precede the box. Each dog individually leaps across the hurdles, hits the release, catches the ball and repeats her path back to the handler. The North American Flyball Association awards titles and maintains statistics.

Backpacking: Backpacking provides an excellent conditioning activity that burns canine energy while you enjoy a healthy hike. Dogs need properly fitted equipment to prevent discomfort and chafing as they carry water, snacks or their own food for overnight trips. Several organizations offer backpacking titles, including the Dog Scouts of America.

Carting: This sport consists of teaching a dog to accept being harnessed, and then pulling a four-wheeled wagon or a two-wheeled sulky. This is related to sledding except that in sledding, the dog runs in a team with other dogs. In carting, the dog may pull by himself or with one other dog.

Weight pulling: This competition allows dogs to pull a heavy sled loaded with weight for a short, measured distance. The competition is divided into weight classifications and the dogs who can pull the heaviest loads in their weight classifications win. This sport requires a dog to be extremely physically fit, with good shoulders and hips, and strong legs. Dogs who excel in this sport can be compared to weight lifters in the human world.

Skijoring: This activity harnesses a dog via a long line to connect him to a person on skis. The skier may hold the long leash in hand, but most people prefer to hold onto one or two ski poles and have the leash hooked to a wide belt around the waist.

Skatejoring: This is ideal for dog owners who enjoy wheeled sports such as inline skating or skateboarding, because it allows them to combine their favorite sport with the husky love of running and pulling. With a leash held in hand, the owner can balance on his or her skates or skateboard while the dog runs and pulls.

United States every year, with more than 100,000 dogs competing. Any registered AKC or UKC dog can enter an obedience trial for the club in which he is registered, regardless of conformational disqualifications or neutering.

Obedience trials are divided into three levels of progressive difficulty. At the first level, Novice, the dogs compete for the title of Companion Dog; at the intermediate level, Open, dogs compete for a Companion Dog Excellent title; and at the Advanced level, dogs compete for a Utility Dog title. Classes are subdivided into "A" (for beginners) and "B" (for more experienced handlers). A perfect score at any level is 200, and a dog must score 170 or better to earn a "leg," three of

which are needed to earn the title. To earn points, the dog must score more than 50 percent of the available points in each exercise; the possible points range from 20 to 40.

Once a dog has earned the Utility Dog title, he can compete with other proven

Agility is a great way to meet other dog owners who have a passion for friendly competition.

obedience dogs for the coveted title of Utility Dog Excellent, which requires that the dog win "legs" in 10 shows. In 1977, the title of Obedience Trial Champion was established by the AKC. Utility Dogs who earn legs in Open B and Utility B earn points toward their Obedience Trial Champion title. To become an OTCh., a dog needs to earn 100 points, which requires three first place wins in Open B and Utility B under three different judges.

The Grand Prix of obedience trials, the AKC National Obedience Invitational, gives qualifying Utility Dogs the chance to win the newest and highest title: National Obedience Champion. Only the top 25 ranked obedience dogs, plus any dog ranked in the top three in his breed, are allowed to compete.

RALLY BEHIND RALLY

Rally is a sport that combines competition obedience with elements of agility, but is less demanding than either one of these activities. Rally was designed keeping the average dog owner in mind and is easier than many other sporting activities.

At a rally event, dogs and handlers are asked to move through 10 to 20 different stations, depending on the level of competition. The stations are marked by numbered signs, which tell the handler the exercise to be performed. The exercises vary from making different types of turns to changing pace.

Dogs can earn rally titles as they get better at the sport and move through the different levels. The titles to strive for are Rally Novice, Rally Advanced, Rally Excellent and Rally Advanced Excellent.

To get your Siberian Husky puppy prepared to enter a rally competition, focus on teaching him basic obedience, for starters. Your dog must know the five basic obedience

cues — sit, down, stay, come and heel — and perform them well. Next, you can enroll your dog in a rally class. Although he must be at least 6 months of age to compete in rally, you can start training long before his 6-month birthday.

SHOW DOGS

When you purchase your Siberian Husky puppy, you must make it clear to the breeder whether you want one just as a lovable companion and pet, or if you hope to purchase a Siberian Husky with show prospects. No reputable breeder will sell you a puppy and tell you that he will definitely be show quality because so much can change during the early months of a puppy's development. If you do plan to show, what you hopefully will have acquired is a puppy with show potential.

To the novice, exhibiting a Siberian Husky in the ring may look easy, but it takes a lot of hard work and devotion to win at a show such as the annual Westminster Kennel Club Dog Show in New York City, not to mention a fair amount of luck, too!

The first concept that the canine novice learns when watching a dog show is that each dog first competes against members of his own breed. Once the judge has selected the best dog in each breed (Best of Breed) the chosen dog will compete with other dogs in his group. Finally, the dogs chosen first in each group will compete for the Best In Show title.

The second concept you must understand is that the dogs are not actually compared against one another. The judge compares each dog against the breed standard, the written description of the ideal dog approved by the AKC or UKC, depending on the sponsoring club. While some early breed standards were indeed based on specific dogs who were famous or popular, many dedicated enthusiasts say that a perfect specimen as described in the standard has never walked into a show ring, has never been bred and, to the woe of dog breeders around the globe, does not exist. Breeders attempt to get as close to this ideal as possible with every litter, but theoretically the "perfect" dog is so elusive that it is impossible. (Even if the perfect dog were born, breeders and judges probably would never agree that he was perfect!)

If you are interested in exploring the world of conformation, your best bet is to join your local breed club or the national (or parent) club, the Siberian Husky Club of America. These clubs often host regional and national specialties, shows only for Siberian Huskies, which can include conformation as well as obedience and field trials. Even if you have no intention of competing with your Siberian Husky, a specialty is like a festival for lovers of the breed who congregate

Siberians don't require a simple sled. Today, there are more outlets to pull, from carts to bicycles.

NOTABLE & QUOTABLE

Getting your Siberian involved in an activity like sledding, skijoring or another sport is an excellent way to exercise him, and it's a lot of fun for you, too. This is a breed who was developed to run more than 60 miles a day; a casual walk around the neighborhood is just not enough. Huskies need owners who are just as adventurous as they are. — Siberian Husky owner Jessica Breinholt from Coalville, Utah

to share their favorite topic: Siberian Huskies! Clubs also send out newsletters, and some organize training days and seminars providing owners the opportunity to learn more about their chosen breed. To locate the breed club closest to you, contact the AKC, which furnishes the rules and regulations for all of these events, plus general dog registration and other basic requirements of dog ownership.

CANINE GOOD CITIZEN

If obedience work sounds too regimented but you'd still like your Siberian Husky to have a title, prepare him for the Canine Good Citizen test. This program is sponsored by the AKC, with tests administered by local dog clubs, private trainers and 4-H clubs.

To earn a CGC title, your Siberian Husky must be well-groomed and demonstrate the manners that all good dogs should exhibit. The CGC test requires a dog to follow the sit, lie down, stay and come cues; react appropriately to other dogs and distractions; allow a stranger to approach him; sit politely for petting; walk nicely on a loose leash; move through a crowd without going wild; calm down after play or praise; and sit still for an examination by the judge. Rules are posted on the AKC's website.

THERAPY

Visiting nursing homes, hospices and hospitals with your dog can be a tremendously satisfying experience. Many times, a dog can reach an individual who has otherwise withdrawn from the world. The Siberian Husky can be a delightful therapy dog. Although a gentle disposition is definitely a plus, the often normally rambunctious dog seems to instinctively become gentler when introduced to those who are weak or ailing. Some basic obedience is, of course,

SMART TIP!

Teaching your Siberian Husky to watch your every move begins when you first bring her home. Puppies will automatically follow you, even without a leash, because they want to be with you, especially if you have a treat in your hand. Keep your dog on your left side and offer her a small piece of food with each step you take. In no time, your Siberian Husky pup will think that you're an automatic treat dispenser, and she will never leave your side.

a necessity for the therapy dog and a repertoire of tricks is a definite bonus.

Most facilities require a dog to have certification from a therapy dog organization. Therapy Dog International and the Delta Society are two such organizations. Generally speaking, if your dog can pass a Canine Good Citizen test, earning certification will not be difficult. Certified therapy dog workers frequently get together a group and regularly make visitations in their area.

NOTABLE & QUOTABLE

Huskies are a working breed. If Huskies aren't given a job, they will become self-employed. Your dog may decide to become a landscaper and dig up the backyard, or your dog may choose to become an interior decorator and tear all the stuffing out of the sofa. — breeder Theresa Przybylski in Crete, Ill.

Smart owners can find out more information about this popular and fascinating breed by contacting the following organizations. They will be glad to help you dig deeper into the world of Siberian Huskies, and you won't even have to beg!

American Kennel Club: The AKC website offers information and links to conformation, tracking, rally, obedience and agility programs, member clubs and all things dog. www.akc.org

Association of American Feed Control Officials: Get the scoop on what's really in your dog's food. www.aafco.org

Canadian Kennel Club: Our northern neighbor's oldest kennel club is similar to the AKC in the states. www.ckc.ca

Canine Performance Events: Sports can keep canines active. www.k9cpe.com

Delta Society: Therapy work is fun and worthwhile, for you, your dog and those people who need extra care. Get involved today! www.deltasociety.org

Dog Scouts of America: Take your dog to camp. www.dogscouts.com

Love on a Leash: Your Siberian has a lot of love to give to others in need. www.loveonaleash.org

it's a
Fact

The **American Kennel Club** was established in 1884. It is America's oldest kennel club. The **United Kennel Club** is the second oldest in the United States and began registering dogs in 1898.

National Association of Professional Pet Sitters: Hire someone to watch your dog. www.petssitters.org

North American Dog Agility Council: This site provides links to clubs, obedience trainers and agility trainers in the United States and Canada. www.nadac.com

North American Flyball Association: Flyball is fun! www.flyball.org

Sled Dog Central: This site has plenty of sledding info. www.sleddogcentral.com

Siberian Husky Club of America: Established in 1938, the SHCA is the AKC-recognized, national breed club for the Siberian Husky. www.shca.org

Therapy Dogs Inc.: Get your husky involved in therapy. www.therapydogs.com

Therapy Dogs International: Find more therapy dog info here: www.tdi–dog.org

United Kennel Club: The UKC offers several of the events offered by the AKC, including agility, conformation and obedience. In addition, the UKC offers competitions in hunting and dog sport (companion and protective events). The UKC, as well as the AKC, offers junior programs. www.ukcdogs.com

United States Dog Agility Association: The USDAA has information on training, clubs and events in the United States, Canada, Mexico, and overseas. www.usdaa.com

World Canine Freestyle Organization: Dancing with your dog is fun! www.world caninefreestyle.org

Don't let your Siberian Husky sit around all day. Get involved in a dog sport.

Plan your vacation to include your Siberian. However, if your destination isn't Fido-friendly, have a good boarding place already lined up.

BOARDING

So you want to take a family vacation — and you want to include all members of the family. You usually make arrangements for accommodations ahead of time anyway, but this is imperative when traveling with a dog. You do not want to make an overnight stop at the only place around for miles only to discover that the hotel doesn't allow dogs. Also, you don't want to reserve a room for your family without confirming that you are traveling with a Siberian Husky because if it is against the hotel's policy, you may not have a place to stay.

Alternatively, if you are traveling and choose not to bring your husky, you will have to make arrangements for him. Some options are to leave him with a family member or a neighbor, have a trusted friend stop by often or stay at your house. Another option is leaving your Siberian Husky at a reputable boarding kennel.

If you choose to board him at a kennel, visit in advance to see the facilities and check how clean they are, and where the dogs are kept. Talk to some of the employees and see how they treat the dogs. Do they spend time with the dogs either during play or exercise? Also, find out the kennel's policy on vaccinations and what they require. This is for all of the dogs' safety because when dogs are kept together, there is a greater risk of diseases being passed between them.

HOME STAFFING

For the husky parent who works all day, a pet sitter or dog walker may be the perfect solution for the lonely pet pooch longing for a midday stroll. Dog owners can contact local high schools or community centers if they don't have a neighbor who is interested in a part-time commitment.

When you interview potential dog walkers, consider their experience with dogs, as well as your husky's rapport with the candidate. You should always thoroughly check all references before entrusting your husky — and opening your home — to a new dog walker.

For an owner's long-term absence, such as a business trip or vacation, many Siberian Husky owners welcome the services of a pet sitter. It's usually less stressful on the dog to stay home with a pet sitter than to be boarded in a kennel. Pet sitters also may be more affordable than a week's stay at a full-service doggie day care.

Pet sitters must be even more reliable than dog walkers because the dog is depending on his surrogate owner for all of his needs over an extended period. Owners are advised to hire a certified pet sitter through the National Association of Professional Pet Sitters. NAPPS provides online and toll-free pet sitter locator services. The nonprofit organization only certifies serious-minded, professional individuals who are knowledgeable in canine behavior, nutrition, health and safety. Whether or not you take your Siberian Husky with you, always keep his best interest at heart when planning a trip.

SCHOOL'S IN SESSION

Puppy kindergarten, which is usually open to dogs between 3 to 6 months of age, allows puppies to learn and socialize with other dogs and people in a structured setting. Classes helps to socialize your Siberian Husky so that he will enjoy going places with you and be a well-behaved member in public gatherings. They prepare him for adult obedience classes and for a lifetime of social experiences he will have with your friends and his furry friends. The problem with most puppy kindergarten classes is that they only occur one night a week.

If you're home during the day, you may be able to find places to take your puppy so he can socialize. Just be careful about dog

- midday meals for young dogs
- obedience training (if offered), using reward-based methods
- safe and comfortable nap areas
- screening of dogs for aggression
- small groups of similar sizes and ages
- toys and playground equipment, such as tunnels and chutes
- trained staff, with an adequate number to supervise the dogs (no more than 10 to 15 dogs per person)
- a webcam

CAR TRAVEL

You should accustom your Siberian Husky to riding in a car at an early age. You may or may not take him in the car often,

parks and other places that are open to any dog. An experience with a dog bully can undo all the good your training classes have done.

If you work, your puppy may be home alone all day, a tough situation for a Siberian Husky. Chances are he can't hold himself that long, so your potty training will be undermined — unless you're teaching him to use an indoor potty. Also, by the time you come home, he'll be bursting with energy, and you may think that he's hyperactive and uncontrollable.

The only suitable answer for the working professional with a Siberian Husky is doggie day care. Most large cities have some sort of day care, whether it's a boarding kennel that keeps your dog in a run or a full-service day care that offers training, play time and even spa facilities. They range from a person who keeps a few dogs at his or her home to a state-of-the-art facility built just for dogs. Many of the more sophisticated doggie day cares offer webcams so you can see what your dog is up to throughout the day. Things to look for:

- escape-proof facilities, such as gates in doorways that lead outside
- inoculation requirements for new dogs

but at the very least he will need to go to the vet once in a while, and you do not want these trips to be traumatic for the dog or troublesome for you. The safest way for a dog to ride in the car is in his crate. If he uses a crate in the house, you can use the same crate for travel.

Don't let your husky go outside without putting on his ID tags.

Another option is a specially made safety harness for dogs, which straps your Siberian Husky in the car much like a seat belt would. Do not let the dog roam loose in the vehicle; this is very dangerous! If you should make an abrupt stop, your dog can be thrown and injured. If your dog starts climbing on you while you are driving, you will not be able to concentrate on the road. It is an unsafe situation for everyone — human and canine.

For long trips, stop often to let your husky relieve himself. Take along whatever you need to clean up after him, including some paper towel should he have an accident in the car or suffer from motion sickness.

IDENTIFICATION

Your Siberian Husky is your valued companion and friend. That is why you always keep a close eye on him, and you have made sure that he cannot escape from the yard or wriggle out of his collar and run away from you. However, accidents can happen and there may come a time when your Siberian Husky unexpectedly gets separated from you. If this should occur, the first thing on your mind will be finding him. Proper identification, including an ID tag, a tattoo and possibly a microchip, will increase the chances of his being returned to you safely and quickly.

An ID tag on a collar or harness is the primary means of identifying a lost pet (and ID licenses are required in many cities). Although inexpensive and easy to read, collars and ID tags can come off or be taken off.

A microchip doesn't get lost. The microchip is embedded underneath the dog's skin and contains a unique ID number that is read by scanners. It comes in handy for identifying lost or stolen pets. However, to be effective, the microchip must be registered in a national database. Smart owners will register their dog and regularly check that their contact information is kept up-to-date.

However, one thing to keep in mind is that not every shelter or veterinary clinic has a scanner, nor do most folks who might pick up and try to return a lost pet.

Your best best? Get both!

INDEX

SIBERIAN HUSKY, a Smart Owner's Guide™
part of the Kennel Club Books® Interactive Series™

JOIN
Club
Husky™
TODAY!

LIBRARY OF CONGRESS CATALOGING-IN-PUBLICATION DATA

Siberian husky / from the editors of Dog fancy magazine.
  p. cm. — (Smart owner's guide)
Includes bibliographical references and index.
ISBN 978-1-59378-775-2
1. Siberian husky. I. Dog fancy (San Juan Capistrano, Calif.)
SF429.S65S515 2010
636.73—dc22

                          2009046641